Enabling Spiritual Care

15 The Chambers, Vineyard
Abingdon OX14 3FE
+44(0)1865 319700 | brf.org.uk

Bible Reading Fellowship (BRF) is a charity (233280)
and company limited by guarantee (301324),
registered in England and Wales

EU Authorised Representative: Easy Access System Europe –
Mustamäe tee 50, 10621 Tallinn, Estonia, **gpsr.requests@easproject.com**

ISBN 978 1 80039 551 0
First published 2026
10 9 8 7 6 5 4 3 2 1 0

Acknowledgements
Pages 130–31: Methodist covenant prayer taken from *The Methodist Worship Book*, copyright Trustees for Methodist Church Purposes 1999. Used with kind permission.

Pages 149–54: Sample memorial services in appendix VI are provided by Anna Chaplain Margaret Hollands and are used with kind permission.

Page 158: Mindfulness exercise is summarised from 'Leaves on a stream' technique in Russ Harris, *ACT Made Simple: An easy-to-read primer on acceptance and commitment therapy* (New Harbinger, 2009), p. 113, used with kind permission (**newharbinger.com**).

Six extracts (pages 66, 125–26, 130, 148, 154) taken from 'Common Worship' © The Archbishops' Council of the Church of England. Used by Permission.

Every effort has been made to trace and contact copyright owners for material used in this resource. We apologise for any inadvertent omissions or errors, and would ask those concerned to contact us so that full acknowledgement can be made in the future.

A catalogue record for this book is available from the British Library.

Printed and bound by CPI Group (UK) Ltd, Croydon CR0 4YY.

Enabling Spiritual Care

A guide for care home staff

Julia Burton-Jones, Catriona Foster,
Sally Rees, and Debbie Thrower

Contents

Introduction

This book is for anyone spending significant time with older people. It is primarily written for staff who work in care homes for older people, drawing from the experiences of Anna Chaplains throughout the UK who work alongside staff teams to offer religious and spiritual care to residents. We hope it will enable care home workers – and others suppprting older people – to understand the distinction between religious and spiritual care, and ways in which every resident (in fact, any one of us when the time comes) benefits from holistic care which nurtures the soul alongside tending to practical, physical, and mental health needs.

The story behind the book

The origins of the book lie within the COVID-19 pandemic, when BRF Ministries published five booklets for care staff to assist them in providing spiritual care during periods when chaplains and other church visitors were unable to offer this face to face during lockdowns. The five booklets have been updated and combined into this single resource and can be found in chapters 2, 3, 5, 6, and 9. Chapters 1, 4, 7, and 8 are new material. During the pandemic, Anna Chaplains bought the booklets and gave them to staff in the homes where they worked so that some of the activities the Anna Chaplains had been offering before lockdown could continue, with staff stepping in to their spiritual care role.

We recognise that visiting chaplains are present in care homes to provide spiritual care for only small periods of time, and that staff are available day and night to identify and respond to the spiritual needs of residents. Clearly, this spiritual role is at its most intense when a resident is dying, but spirituality is a core element of the well-being we seek for each older person living in a care setting each day.

Recognising the continuing need for spiritual care resourcing for staff, BRF Ministries decided to update the guides created in the pandemic and produce a book aimed at the care home workforce. We hope and pray it will resource staff in their spiritual care responsibilities and give them confidence in having conversations with residents about their sources of meaning and purpose in life. Where residents hold religious beliefs, whatever their faith, we hope staff will feel empowered to seek appropriate input from faith communities in meeting their needs.

The role of Anna Chaplains

Anna Chaplains are Christians appointed by their churches to offer spiritual support to older people. They help older people who have a Christian faith to continue practising their faith when frailty makes participation in church life challenging. Anna Chaplains also make connections with older people who have no church background, accompanying them spiritually through conversations about the deep things of life and what is important to them. Some Anna Chaplains are in paid roles, but most are volunteers. They are carefully recruited by their churches, with relevant enhanced DBS checks and vulnerable adults safeguarding training.

Anna Chaplains offer spiritual and religious care both in one-to-one encounters and in groups. They may pray with individual residents who are Christians or simply befriend a resident who is lonely and values a heart-to-heart with someone who cares. They may hold a regular church service in the care home or offer craft activities, singing groups, or reminiscence sessions, depending on their skills and interests, as well as what will benefit the care home community. No two Anna Chaplains work in the same way, and they aim to collaborate with senior staff and activity coordinators to identify ways of working that are appropriate.

Who is this resource written for and how might it be used?

Enabling Spiritual Care is primarily aimed at those working in care homes, including managers, senior staff, carers, and activity/well-being coordinators. Other care home staff, and indeed homecare workers, may also find it of interest in developing approaches to person-centred care. Relatives and friends of care home residents may find it of value in considering the spiritual and religious care needs of their relative/ friend, perhaps even using some of the resources outlined here (particularly those found in the appendices of this book). Groups who may also be interested are Anna Chaplains, church workers involved in care home ministry, and chaplains in other settings working with older people, such as hospital chaplains.

This is a book you can dip into as circumstances dictate. There is no need to read it from cover to cover, but having a sense of the structure may help put chapter headings in context. The appendices have resources you can make use of straightaway. Some chapters may help new staff understand spiritual needs, others may be of value to activity and well-being coordinators in planning religious and spiritual care, and linking with local churches.

The book aims to assist care home staff in identifying and collaborating with faith communities who might work alongside them in responding to religious and spiritual needs of residents. We hope that fruitful collaborations with local churches will contribute to the spiritual well-being of all residents in care homes, not only those who are Christians.

Distinguishing between religious and spiritual care

There is a common confusion about what is religious and what is spiritual care, and a misunderstanding that religious care equals spiritual care. This can lead to confusion in assessing and meeting spiritual and religious care needs of residents.

Religious care is easier to recognise than spiritual care, and commonly other people (priests, ministers, and church members) come in to give this care, particularly for services of worship, Holy Communion, and end-of-life care. In this book, some chapters focus on religious care, such as chapters 2 and 3, which are about worship and prayer for Chrisitan residents. Other chapters are more broadly focused on spirituality, such as chapter 8 on creative approaches.

Care staff are not always familiar with the concept of 'spirituality', but they may know what holistic care is (about the whole person rather than just body and mind) and be frustrated at times that in a pressured care home environment the physical needs often take priority. They may also be familiar with 'person-centred care', so that focusing on the whole person – their personality, the person 'inside', which includes their past, present, and future – is how they seek to provide care; they understand that grasping aspects of the person's family and work life, their hobbies, and what is important to them is vital in building a picture of them as a unique individual and creating a complete care plan that evolves over time. This book builds on and develops notions of holistic and person-centred care to unpick what might be core to a person's identity in terms of faith, beliefs, and spirituality.

The entire staff team in a care home fulfils a role in meeting spiritual needs, while perhaps not recognising it. Every conversation between a resident and staff member where there is a meeting of hearts is a spiritual conversation. Talking with residents about their feelings and desires meets spiritual needs. Attending to the individual personal care wishes of each person affirms their identity and sense of self, so reinforcing the self in a spiritual way. Cultivating the garden so it is an oasis of peace meets spiritual needs. Providing meals that observe religious requirements also contributes to good spiritual and religious care.

The drive and passion of care workers to provide the best quality of life for older people in their final years is what motivates them to ensure spiritual and religious needs are met. To pray with someone for whom prayer is a comfort and reassurance may feel uncomfortable, but knowing it will bring relief to an anxious soul is reason enough to overcome embarrassment.

Attending to our own spiritual needs

Another aspiration in producing this book is that the reader will become better attuned to their own spirituality, more aware of, and better able to meet, their own spiritual needs. Working with frail older people in care homes is immensely rewarding but also emotionally and spiritually demanding at times. Staff can be stretched to the limits; space to rest and reflect during taxing shifts is in short supply. Working with distressed residents going through tremendous loss and change requires empathy and compassion and can be draining, carrying with it a risk of burnout.

Chapter 9 is about self-care. Initially written during the pandemic when staff were experiencing unprecedented stress and trauma, it holds value still for hard-working and committed care home workers. For some, the trauma of COVID-19 has not passed, and there are regular reminders of the intolerable pressures.

The role of Anna Chaplains includes spiritual care for staff and visitors, not just residents. They hope to be a source of care and support for staff members who may be struggling with personal difficulties or grieving, perhaps for a resident they were close to who has died. Some care homes have arranged for their Anna Chaplains to provide times dedicated to staff, where space is provided for private conversations and a little pampering.

What is religious and spiritual care, and how do we meet needs?

Julia Burton-Jones

In this chapter we will explore what is meant by spiritual care and how it differs from, but might incorporate, religious care. We aim to show that, while not everyone has religious needs, we all have spiritual needs which are addressed by offering holistic (whole-person) care.

When is spiritual care needed?

We need it all the time! When a carer brushes a frail resident's hair, for example, and makes sure the parting is on their preferred side, so that the person looks as they normally do – arguably, that's spiritual care. Their identity is being valued.

If you make time to listen to someone telling you a little about their earlier life, you are honouring that individual and making them feel special and unique – that's spiritual care, too. So, a lot of spiritual care is what you are already doing instinctively, as time allows.

Each of us copes with challenging periods of our lives in different ways. We resort to the things we like doing best when times are tough – such as walking in the park, gardening, watching a film, listening to our favourite music, reading, or doing something creative like knitting or baking. These are things that we do when we need to recharge our batteries and ensure our minds are absorbed in something pleasurable. All those activities constitute good spiritual *self*-care.

How do we make sure we offer that to residents as well? Activities coordinators, for instance, are key to a well-run care home because they can nurture the spirit of people by offering a variety of activities, especially once individuals are living in residential care and are less able to choose how they spend their time themselves.

Opportunities to choose your own hobbies and pastimes become limited when you move into care. It is a case of fitting in with the timetable of the home. There has to be a well-organised routine if a home is going to provide safe and effective care for all. Yet the individual needs of one person, as well as those of others, must also be considered. One resident might love a certain type of classical music, say, while another enjoys a loud TV programme, and so the needs of both have to be catered for and balanced.

The idea that health includes more than physical health, and that there is a relationship between spiritual and physical well-being, has been understood for centuries in terms of balance, inner peace, and having a sense of purpose and meaning.

To enjoy well-being in later life, indeed at any stage of life, you need to be fed, clothed, housed, and have access to medical treatment. Once our basic needs have been met, we also crave company, love, attention, and to be surrounded by the possessions and resources which matter to us most.

Understanding spiritual and religious care

Are spiritual and religious care different, and if so, how might we define them? A good definition comes from NHS Scotland:

> Religious care is given in the context of the shared religious beliefs, values, liturgies and lifestyle of a faith community. Spiritual care is usually given in a one-to-one relationship, is completely person-centred and makes no assumptions about personal conviction or life orientation.

> Spiritual care is not necessarily religious. Religious care, at its best, should always be spiritual.
>
> 'Spiritual care and chaplaincy', The Scottish Government, 2009

Who is responsible for providing spiritual and religious care?

Religious care provision

Some religious charities provide care homes for people of particular faiths. MHA is one of the largest care home groups and is run by the Methodist Church, for instance, and Jewish Care is a provider of care for Jewish people. Some care home groups with a religious foundation are open to anyone willing to live in a place run on faith principles, regardless of their own beliefs, as is the case often with faith-based schools. In other contexts, residents all share the same faith. In these faith-based homes, the provision of religious care is an integral part of the service, so it is usually provided in-house by the faith community.

Most care homes, however, are not run by religious organisations, meaning the way in which religious care is offered differs. Staff still have a responsibility to enable religious care needs to be met, but they will rarely be meeting them directly. Under equality legislation, religion is a protected characteristic, often linked to cultural needs; there is a duty to ensure a person's religion is accommodated in the provision of care. Usually this means enabling the person to maintain links with their religious community and allowing representatives of that faith group to visit the person in fulfilling the rites and rituals of the faith.

While we may not get involved in the religious practices of a faith group to which we do not belong, we can support a resident who is a member of that faith group in living their life according to their beliefs. They may rely on staff to help with mobility, for instance, and being able to move to a part of the home where they can pray or read sacred texts that are part of their religion. There may be dietary requirements and items of clothing and jewellery that hold religious significance. Learning about the person's beliefs is not only interesting and enriching, it also helps us provide care sensitively and respectfully. Members of the person's faith group and perhaps an Anna Chaplain are best placed to signpost sources of information about their worldview and lifestyle, and might be willing to offer guidance to staff.

Although we recognise that there are many forms of worship and religious care, this book focuses on Christian worship.

Spiritual care provision

Spiritual care is different from religious care in that it can be part of all aspects of the resident's life, from getting up in the morning to going to bed at night. As mentioned earlier, paying attention to the person's appearance in how you support grooming and dressing is a way of honouring their identity. Learning about the person's interests and what gives them comfort and joy might enable you to be someone who can lift their spirits on a difficult day.

Every member of staff can play a part in spiritual care, not just care staff. Through the conversations they have and how they contribute to the well-being of residents, there is the potential for each colleague to enrich the spiritual lives of residents. Friends and family members also meet spiritual needs, especially for love, a sense of belonging, and being needed. Residents can also care for one another in ways that nurture their sense of self. Of course, volunteers from the local community, including church visitors and chaplains, are also involved in meeting spiritual needs.

If you do not know what support your resident needs, it should be easy to find out. Most residents will have a care plan in which spiritual and religious needs should be noted. If this information is not available, then simply ask the older person whether they would like to have a time of worship or prayer and see what they say.

Spiritual distress

Spiritual distress is a concept widely understood in palliative care. It is apparent when a person is clearly in pain, but the source is not physical. Spiritual pain is sometimes called 'existential' pain/crisis and is linked to a person's life story, the people, places, events, and experiences that have given their life meaning and purpose.

The person in spiritual distress may be struggling to come to terms with what their life has held, and they may be experiencing intense anger, guilt, loneliness, and emptiness. They may be afraid of dying. They may feel that they are a burden to their families. Providing comfort and relief in this distress might mean offering help in healing a broken relationship, dealing with unfinished business, or helping the person with religious practices that bring peace.

Puzzling behaviours

As the brain is progressively damaged in dementia, it can cause changes in behaviour which sometimes leave family members and care home staff baffled. The person may be unable to explain the reasons for these strange behaviour patterns, but we know the onus is on those who care for the person to understand, particularly when the changes are accompanied by distress. Clinical psychologists work with complex cases of behaviour change in dementia where others have struggled to uncover the causes. One such psychologist is Graham Stokes, who has written fascinating books explaining the sometimes-tortuous processes through which he and his team found the reasons for a behaviour.

In his book *And Still the Music Plays* (Hawker Publications, 2008), he tells the story of a care home resident with dementia who he calls Mrs D. Mrs D refuses to stay in her room, even at night-time. The puzzle is solved when Stokes discovers she is a devout Catholic. Her bedroom walls are painted purple, which in Catholicism is the colour associated with death, grief, and mourning, thus sparking an intense sense of dread in Mrs D when taken to her room. When her bedroom walls are painted green, she happily settles, and this puzzling behaviour stops immediately!

Mrs D is a good example of someone whose changed behaviour is linked to spiritual and religious identity. In considering potential reasons for strange patterns of behaviour, it helps to consider faith and spirituality as a potential influence.

Regulatory requirements in meeting spiritual and religious needs

Each nation of the UK has its own regulatory framework for health and social care under which care homes are inspected:

- Care Inspectorate Wales
- Care Inspectorate, Healthcare Improvement Scotland
- Regulation and Quality Improvement Authority for Northern Ireland
- Care Quality Commission (England)

In searching for standards that have a bearing on faith and spirituality, we might pick out references to 'things that matter to the person' or 'purposeful activities', and to faith, culture, indeed human rights. It is notable how few explicit references can be found to 'spirituality' or 'spiritual needs' in the current requirements; however, both are implied where the wishes and voice of the service user are mentioned, and where personalised care which respects the individual is expected. In appendix IX, each nation's requirements in relation to spiritual and religious care are set out (page 163).

Here are some examples of how religious and spiritual needs are covered in the regulations:

- The regulations mention religion, culture, and spirituality in the context of needs assessment and creating personalised care plans. A care home might be deemed unsuitable for an older person if it is unable to meet religious and spiritual needs.

- Religion and culture are considered in the context of protected equality characteristics, firmly enshrined in human rights and protection against discrimination.
- There is also provision for residents to maintain their links with community, friends and family, and people who are important to them. This may include their faith community.
- Standards refer to the need for independence, choice, and control over the lifestyle residents establish in the care home, so they can continue to live in ways that are meaningful to them. There is mention of personal goals and aspirations which may include a sense of the spiritual and religious.
- Dignity and respect are pillars of the standards for each nation, and respect for faith and culture is included in these principles.
- The programme of events and activities is expected to be purposeful and to be age- and culturally appropriate, planned with the interests of residents in mind and taking into account their spiritual needs.
- How food and drink are provided should also reference cultural needs.
- End-of-life plans should be documented to include cultural and religious wishes, and when the person dies, any necessary rituals and treatment of the body are to be organised in accordance with these wishes.

Safeguarding

Failing to meet religious and spiritual needs may fall into the category of abuse. One form of abuse is discriminatory abuse. This is abuse based on a protected characteristic under the Equality Act 2010, which includes religion and belief. It might be verbal abuse, derogatory remarks, or inappropriate language related to the person's religion and beliefs. Or it could be exclusion or substandard service provision or unequal treatment relating to the protected characteristic.

Neglect is another area of abuse which could be experienced by a resident whose religious or spiritual needs were unmet. This might be failure to provide the diet a person's religion requires, or not supporting them in personal care, for instance with ablution rituals in Islam before prayer.

In conclusion

Our spirituality is the core of our being, the essence of who we are as a unique human. Good care seeks to discover the person behind the diagnoses of long-term health conditions that may have led to the individual being admitted to full-time care.

Good care nurtures the soul and lifts the spirit as well as tending to the body. We see some facets of spiritual identity reflected in religious faith and cultural heritage, but it includes the broader desires and goals a person holds, linking to what brings them hope and comfort in times of difficulty, and where their sense of strength and resilience lies.

Documenting spiritual needs requires more than ticking boxes stating a person's religion and what they want to happen when they die. It may take time to add colour and depth to the spiritual dimensions of a care plan, but when this process is developed it shows the person as they truly wish to be seen by those with responsibility for their care.

Case study

Josie

Josie is passionate about the environment and looking after the world's resources. She worked as a primary school teacher and loves to tell stories about the joy and amazement of her pupils when she took them on nature walks and they discovered and learned about plants and insects.

She worries about the planet and the damage humanity has done to many species through disrespecting nature. Worrying about the harm being done through global warming keeps her awake at night. Before her stroke she was part of an allotment project where children from disadvantaged communities learned about growing vegetables and the bigger picture of conservation work. She continues to support several conservation charities with small but regular donations. She loves to watch nature documentaries and longs for the days when most of her spare time was spent outdoors. She is quite an 'evangelist' over recycling and wants to know how it is being practised in the care home.

Josie thrives in the company of young people. Her earnest hope for the future is that the world they inherit is protected from environmental harms and they are staunch defenders of the natural world. In this she is optimistic, seeing much that gives her hope in the attitudes and aspirations of children and adolescents she meets.

Josie's spirituality – *Josie's spirituality may not include religious beliefs, but she holds strongly to a set of values around caring for the planet and nurturing young people. This gives her meaning and purpose in life. Her hope for the future is a better world for the next generations.*

Questions to help in assessing spiritual and religious needs of the older person

The Spiritual Care Series training resource for churches offering spiritual care to older people is a course provided by BRF Ministries in the UK (see **annachaplaincy.org.uk/spiritual-care-series**). It has a bank of questions for a spiritual care assessment based on four key questions. It is not suggested all the questions are asked straightaway when a person moves into a care home, but they may help if used over a period of time in teasing out spiritual identity and need. These questions might be helpful in one-to-one conversations but could also form the basis of interesting small-group discussions which enable residents to get to know each other.

The four key questions are:

1 Who am I?
2 Where do I come from?
3 Where am I going?
4 Why?

Under each of these questions, there are conversation topics aimed at enabling the older person to express their spiritual needs, of which a selection are listed here.

Who am I?

- How do you connect with others (family, friends, community carers)?
- What are your sources of hope, strength, comfort, peace, and joy?
- What do you believe in or have faith in?
- Are there things you struggle with now?

Where do I come from?

- Looking back over your life, what do you remember with sadness and what do you remember with joy?
- What do you hold on to during difficult times – what sustains you and helps to keep you going?
- What has been your faith journey?
- Are you fearful of anything? If so, what triggers these fears?

Where am I going?

- What do you value in life that you still want to continue with?
- Do you belong to a spiritual/faith community?
- What aspects of your spirituality would you like us to be aware of as we care for you?
- Going forward, what spiritual goals do you want to explore or grow into?

Why?

- What brings meaning in your life?
- Are you hopeful? What do you hope for, and why?
- What do you want from life?
- What is really important to you now and in the future?

How to facilitate Christian worship with individuals in your care

The Revd Sally Rees

All individuals are different, so we have provided several suggestions that can be 'mixed and matched' for the older person in your care. They vary in style to suit different tastes, from informal to more formal times of worship. You can choose just one or two worship activities, or perhaps a short service. Examples are given in appendix V (page 139). We suggest that the time spent in individual worship could be five minutes, or longer if the resident is engaging in a beneficial way.

What does individual worship look like?

- Creating a quiet space for worship
- Worshipping as part of creation
- Singing hymns and songs
- Individual worship through reading Bible verses
- Reflecting on a Bible verse or hymn
- Individual worship and prayer
- Creative worship
- Connecting with others in the church family

Creating a quiet space for worship

Sometimes just creating a quiet space in the older person's room is all that is needed. This can be done fairly easily if you have near the older person a flat surface, like a table, stool, or lap tray, on which you can put symbols found in a church.

These are some of the things that someone might like to see:

- A white covering, such as a napkin, a hanky, or a pillowcase. Alternatively, you could designate a cushion as a special 'prayer cushion'.
- A cross, such as a wooden cross or a picture of a cross that the person has in their room already. A palm cross (from Easter) or a cross on a neck chain can also be used. Any cross can be used, but there is such a thing as a 'holding cross'; some people like to hold a cross to help them focus.
- A candle. If a naked flame is not appropriate, use battery-powered tea-lights or candles.
- A Bible, a New Testament (their own, if possible, but most homes have a copy somewhere), or perhaps a Book of Common Prayer.
- A small vase of flowers.
- Rosaries or prayer beads are, likewise, a helpful guide for focusing on prayer for some people.

This might be all that the older person needs to be quiet with God and to feel close to him in the silence of prayer and contemplation. Stay with the person and share the silence and God's presence if you can.

Worshipping as part of creation

Some people feel God's presence more easily outside. If you can take your older person outside even for 15 minutes, this can be a refreshing time of worship. It may not be silent, as there might be sounds of the breeze in the trees, birdsong, or other people's voices; nevertheless, it can still be worship.

Singing hymns and songs

Singing is really good for the soul, and many older people can join in with gusto with hymns and songs that they know. They have sung many of these hymns from their youth and they have become part of the fabric of their very being. Try to find out what their favourites are.

Sometimes you can just sing known hymns and choruses together. Most older people are familiar with these hymns (see appendix I, page 109, for the words)

- ‘All things bright and beautiful’
- ‘Amazing grace’
- ‘He’s got the whole world in his hands’
- ‘Be thou my vision’
- ‘Jesus loves me – this I know’
- ‘Jesus bids us shine with a pure, clear light’

These songs can almost immediately bring heartfelt joy and help a person remember and feel God’s presence close to them.

If you do not know the tune or the words of a hymn the older person wants to sing, you might well find that they have some CDs with hymns or praise songs that you could listen to and sing along with together. In Wales, quite a few older people have CDs of male voice choirs or featuring Aled Jones or Catherine Jenkins. There will often be some hymns on these.

Sometimes, people will remember only the first verse of a hymn or the chorus line. There is no need to sing all the verses; just sing the words that your resident knows and listen to the rest.

If there are no CDs available, and you have access to the internet, there are hundreds of hymns and choruses on YouTube or other music-streaming apps, such as Spotify. If you use a smartphone, you can play the hymn or song on that or use a Bluetooth speaker.

There are also lots of resources available for purchase. Some of these are listed in appendix I (page 109).

If you need any help with this, please feel free to contact your local Anna Chaplain, minister, or pastoral visitor.

Individual worship through reading Bible verses

Many older people know many Bible verses, such as:

> For God so loved the world, that he gave his only begotten Son, that whosoever believeth in him should not perish, but have everlasting life.
> JOHN 3:16 (KJV)

> This is the day which the Lord hath made; we will rejoice and be glad in it.
> PSALM 118:24 (KJV)

> The Lord is my light and my salvation; whom shall I fear? The Lord is the strength of my life; of whom shall I be afraid?
> PSALM 27:1 (KJV)

Some, but by no means all, will prefer the 'old-fashioned' version of the Bible called the King James Version (KJV), but any reading of Bible verses and Bible stories will warm the heart and soul.

Many older people know by heart familiar psalms, such as Psalm 23 ('The Lord is my shepherd') and Psalm 121 ('I lift up my eyes to the mountains'). If you are able to start a familiar psalm, especially Psalm 23, you may find that they will be able to recite it all.

However, no one can be expected to know a number of Bible verses by heart, so ask your older friend whether they have a Bible, a New Testament, Book of Common Prayer, or similar worship book, from which you can read together. Read a psalm which is likely to be familiar, for example Psalm 23, 27, 121, or 139. Each of these can be found in appendix II (page 115).

There are also many wonderful stories in the Bible. Two of the shorter books in the Old Testament are stories of two individual people – Jonah and Ruth. The New Testament is full of stories that Jesus told and stories of people Jesus met, such as Zacchaeus (Luke 19:1–10) or

Peter and Andrew (Matthew 4:18–22). If you look in any of the gospels (Matthew, Mark, Luke, and John), you will find a good story with a message that your resident is likely to know.

Reflecting on a Bible verse or hymn

Some people like to pause to think for a little time after reading the Bible, so that they can listen to what God might be saying to them from the verses that were read.

BRF Ministries has excellent resources, such as *Bible Reflections for Older People*, which is published three times a year. Each page has a Bible verse, a short reflection, and a prayer that can be used and would take about ten minutes to read and reflect upon.

There are several free apps or email devotionals that have a short service and/or Bible readings and reflections, such as 'Pray As You Go', 'Sacred Space', and Premier's 'Be Still and Know'.

Ask your chaplain or other visitor from the local church to tell you about resources that they may be able to supply.

Case study

Kwame

Kwame was born in Ghana into a Christian family. From his early years he read the Bible every day and spent time in prayer. This familiar and reassuring routine was a source of strength in the huge upheaval of moving to the UK in his 30s. He clung on to the promises of God which he read in the Bible.

Kwame moved to Maple Court care home from the local hospital; following a serious fall, it was decided he could no longer live safely in his flat, which was on the third floor of an apartment building. His niece who helped with the move did not think to include his

Bible in the possessions she brought for him when he moved into Maple Court. When Kwame realised it was missing, he was distressed. Seeing how important his Bible was to Kwame, deputy manager Carol contacted his niece Amma to ask if she might go back to the flat and retrieve it. Kwame visibly relaxed when Amma brought the Bible and placed it on the table by his bed.

Individual worship and prayer

Prayer is the way we talk to and listen to God. Prayer can be silent, but many people are more comfortable when they pray out loud.

Many older people know some prayers by heart, especially the Lord's Prayer (found in appendix III, page 125–26).

But there are many others, such as:

- The Serenity Prayer
- The Grace
- The Aaronic blessing.

These can be found in appendix III (page 125).

Prayer is quite simply talking to God – so anyone can do it. Take the plunge and try, even if you feel self-conscious to begin with. Sometimes you will find that the person will pray for you, which is a wonderful experience.

Creative worship

Many older people love to be creative and regard creativity as a form of worship. Making something that connects a person with God, with their church family or with those in need is worship. Examples of this are:

- Prayer shawls – some churches have schemes that encourage older people to knit, for example, shawls for new, young mothers in their church families, and to pray for them as they do so.
- Some older people knit squares that can be made into a blanket for someone in need, at home or abroad.
- Some older people knit hats for premature babies in special care units in their local hospitals.

Not everyone likes, or is able, to knit, but there are many craft activities that can be used as creative worship:

- Colouring a bookmark or postcard, especially if it contains a Bible verse.
- Writing kind words on a card and sending it to a friend.

There are also many activities that can be associated with worship. BRF Ministries has more suggestions on the Messy Vintage webpage (**messychurch.org.uk/messy-vintage**). The activity part of a Messy Vintage service can be enough to help a person to worship and to connect with God. There is an example activity outline for Messy Vintage in appendix III (page 133).

Connecting with others in the church family

Helping an individual to practise their faith is important but, for many, joining in with others is also really helpful. Chapter 3 gives ideas on worshipping with a group of residents, but group worship is not easy for everyone.

If your resident has a radio or a television, there are some lovely worship programmes, especially on a Sunday, for example:

- BBC Radio 4, *Sunday Worship* at 8.10 am
- BBC One, *Songs of Praise*, usually 1.15 pm or 1.30 pm

There is at least one daily service each weekday on the radio, such as:

- BBC Radio 4 Extra at 9.45 am

If you or the older person in your care has access to the internet, there are many services online, such as via YouTube. There may well be a service online from the older person's local church – it's worth a look.

Finally, for those who are not on the internet, there is an alternative source of worship:

- DailyHOPE is a telephone service that was established during the COVID-19 pandemic for older people who may struggle to connect with a church service online. It continues still, and by phoning 0345 646 2206 you can choose to be put through to hymns, prayers, and reflections 24 hours a day.

In conclusion

For some older people in your care, a regular pattern of praying and reading the Bible has been an essential part of life, without which they would feel bereft. Support to continue these routines forms a key element of effective care. Religious and spiritual practices are not just 'nice to have'; they are essential, and bring comfort, hope, and peace at a time of life when there is change and loss. We have explored what this means for residents who are Christians, but prayer, worship, and reading holy books is important in other faiths, too, and can be facilitated with sensitivity and respect.

How to enable Christian worship with a group of residents

Catriona Foster

In this chapter, we will look at how you can hold your own mini church service with some of your residents. You may choose to do this because an Anna Chaplain, minister, priest, or other church visitor is unable to. For example, if a local church or chaplain visits once a month to hold a services, you might want to hold a service between their visits.

Worshipping together as a group is important for Christians – it is one aspect of practising their faith. So having a group worship time in the care home means that those who regularly went to church before becoming housebound won't miss out. They will feel that church is coming to them when they are no longer able to go out to church. Other residents, who perhaps weren't used to attending church, might also like to join in and may appreciate the encouragement, prayers, and fellowship of these special times together.

Group worship

If someone on the staff team attends a church, perhaps they could lead the service, but even if you've never been to church, you can still help the residents with this activity. You might like to use the three sample services in appendix V (page 139). If you have someone who normally leads a service in your care home, you could ask them for ideas of Bible verses, prayers, and so on.

Be flexible

Every care home is different. For example, they will differ in terms of the degree of frailty of the residents and in the number of residents living with dementia. This chapter will give you some ideas, but you will want to do what works for you and your residents.

Your worship service can be very informal. It might include laughter (or tears) and noise (or silence). It might include passing an object round or doing an activity. You will have to spend a bit of time beforehand planning and preparing what you are going to do. Short and simple is always best. Don't forget that if you have an Anna Chaplain or other regular church visitor, they may have resources you can use.

What might a service look like?

Group worship could include some of the following:

- Setting the scene
- Opening words
- Singing
- Bible reading
- Time of reflection
- Prayers
- A blessing

It can be helpful to have a 'theme' for each service – a simple word or phrase that you can base the service around, for example:

- Thanking God for beauty in nature
- Peace
- Loving and caring for one another
- Thanksgiving for our food/Harvest
- Seasons
- Laughter
- Loss

Setting the scene

When you are ready to start, is there anything you could do to help the residents focus on a time of worship? For example:

- Set up a small table with a cloth, a battery-operated candle, and a vase of flowers on it.
- Setting up a cross on the table is good, if you have one – or you could draw a basic cross and use sticky tack to attach it to the front of the table.
- Play some quiet hymn music in the background.
- Is there a Bible you could show and then put on the table?

Opening words

You can begin the service with words that draw people together and help them to focus on God. For example:

> The Lord is here and his Spirit is with us.

Or use the following Bible verses:

> [Jesus said,] 'Where two or three are gathered together in my name, there am I in the midst of them.'
> **MATTHEW 18:20 (KJV)**

> Draw near to God, and he will draw near to you.
> **JAMES 4:8**

Singing

Singing is a great group activity which helps people to engage and to have a sense of togetherness. Some of the residents will remember old hymns from many years ago – the words and tunes can touch them in deep ways, reaching the parts others cannot reach. Singing is also like a 'tool' that helps us to worship God.

It might be difficult to sing some hymns and songs together if you don't have a musician or if you don't know the songs yourself. However, here are some ideas that might work:

- One of the residents might be able to start singing the verse of a hymn, which others can then join in with.
- It's possible to sing a simple well-known song without music – try, if you know it, 'He's got the whole world in his hands'.
- Choose a hymn or two (see below, or ask a resident for a choice beforehand), then find the tune online and have it ready to play when you need it. Alternatively, you could use a CD of hymn tunes.
- It's often best to sing the first verse only of a hymn – some of the residents will remember the words of the first verse. You could sing that one verse twice over.
- If you stick to the first verse only of very well-known hymns, you may not need words. Alternatively, you could print off some words beforehand for the residents.
- Make a joyful noise! Do actions or clap or use shakers for percussion – if that fits with the song. Encourage singing from the heart, with feeling!

Popular hymns and songs, for which you will find the words in appendix I (page 109), include:

- 'He's got the whole world in his hands'
- 'All things bright and beautiful'
- 'Jesus loves me, this I know'
- 'Amazing grace'
- 'The Lord's my shepherd'
- 'The old rugged cross'
- 'What a friend we have in Jesus'
- 'Be thou my vision'

Bible reading

This is an important part of the worship service. Read aloud just one verse or a short passage from the Bible. Have your verse(s) ready to read, either from a Bible or printed out from the internet (**biblegateway.com** may help you here). Here are some you could choose:

- Joshua 1:9
- Psalm 23
- Psalm 46:1–3, 10–11
- Psalm 121
- John 15:12
- Philippians 4:4–7

Time of reflection

Take some time in the service to help the residents to reflect on the Bible verse or the theme, for example:

- Pass something round, such as some autumn leaves, an acorn, a beautiful feather, a lump of melting snow(!), an ornament, or something precious – anything that links with the theme or inspires a sense of wonder. As you show it to each resident in turn, take time to let them touch it and comment on it.
- Staff could help the residents do a simple craft activity that links with the service, such as making a flower out of tissue paper. This could be done before, during, or after the service.
- Can you think of a little story that fits with the Bible verse? For instance, was there a time when you got lost? (The Bible says God is with you wherever you go.) Was there a time when you were particularly anxious? (God gives us peace.) Alternatively, talk about what makes you happy (giving thanks).

Prayers

Invite the residents to join in saying the Lord's Prayer together (see appendix III, page 125–26).

Perhaps you could then say a one-sentence prayer based on the theme ('Thank you, God, that you understand our sadness; help us to know that you are close to us') or say one of the prayers in appendix III (page 125). You could also ask if anyone has something specific they would like to thank God for, or pray for, then list these in a simple prayer ('Dear God, please help George to feel better… Thank you for Jose's new great-grandson… Please help Barbara's knees to be better… We join with Alisha in asking for peace in the world. Amen').

A blessing

Bring your service to a close by asking for God's blessing on your residents and yourself (see the sample services in appendix V (page 139) for words you can use). After a general blessing, you could even go around the group and bless each resident by name – see appendix V (page 148) for an example.

Top tips

- As with any communal activity in the care home, you will need to speak loudly so that as many of the group as possible can hear.
- Using the residents' names and drawing them in when appropriate as you go along can help to keep them engaged ('Iris, you used to grow roses in your garden, didn't you?'; 'Hassan, I remember you telling me you used to kick the autumn leaves on your way to school').

- Try not to rush the service. Give the residents time to pause and reflect.
- Special times of the year can be used as themes in your worship service – Harvest (in the autumn), Remembrance Day, Christmas, New Year, St Valentine's Day, Easter, and so on.
- Remember, if you have one, your Anna Chaplain or church visitor can support you in all this.

In conclusion

Bringing residents together for a time of worship can be a great comfort and encouragement to them. For those who have attended church every week throughout their lives, this is a routine and a ritual that holds great significance. It can provide stability and continuity at a time of change and challenge. Connections between residents may be formed as they recognise in one another kindred spirits. They can form their own church congregation in the care home.

Holy Communion and other rites in the Christian faith

Julia Burton-Jones

All religions have traditions, customs, practices, and rituals which are important for those who hold to that faith. Respecting these ways of expressing faith is important in offering person-centred care. Religious practices are an essential part of a person's identity and give them a sense of belonging and connection, both to their community and a higher being.

'Religion, belief or lack of belief' is a protected characteristic under the Equality Act 2010, which protects people from discrimination. The other protected characteristics covered by the legislation are: age; disability; gender reassignment; marriage and civil partnership; pregnancy and maternity; race; sex; sexual orientation. The Equality Act 2010 provides a legal basis for challenging discrimination based on religious belief, which might include not being supported in faith practices.

In inspecting care homes, regulatory bodies look at how well religious and cultural needs are being met for residents. As we noted in chapter 1, the CQC regulatory framework for England, for example, considers how residents' needs are being met under the heading of 'caring' and includes a quality statement:

> We treat people as individuals and make sure their care, support and treatment meets their needs and preferences. We take account of their strengths, abilities, aspirations, culture and unique backgrounds and protected characteristics.

To meet religious needs for Christian residents, it helps to understand the faith practices which have been fundamental to a resident's way of life. It is essential to respect faith practices of residents of other faiths, too, linking with local faith leaders to learn about the traditions of those from other religious backgrounds and what can be done to support their beliefs and practices.

Chapter 8 explains some of the differences between Christian denominations. A Roman Catholic Christian will practise their faith in ways that may differ from a Methodist Christian, for example, while central beliefs are commonly held across denominations ('denomination' is the generic name for a branch of the Christian church). Certain rituals shared across many Christian groups are practised in slightly different ways. It is impossible to cover all the variations in this short guide, but we will introduce some of the faith practices your residents may consider important, their underlying meanings, and implications for care planning.

The Trinity – God as three in one

In common with most world religions, Christians believe in a divine presence and seek to love, worship, and obey their God as the creator and sustainer of the world. Christians believe that God is one God made up of three persons – God the Father, God the Son (Jesus), and God the Holy Spirit.

Prayer

Prayer and meditation are part of most world religions. In Christianity, a person's relationship with God is expressed through prayer. Put simply, Christians see God as a person with whom they have a relationship. Just as they would talk to a friend or family member, they talk to God. This is a two-way communication in which the believer perceives God's response – sometimes as a voice, but in other ways too, such as through something significant that another person says, or through significant texts, or even through pictures. This is what Christians call prayer. It might be a short 'please, help me' prayer, or a longer time of reflection. Sometimes Christians pray in their own words, and sometimes they use prayers from the Bible (see below) or say prayers that have been written by someone else.

The best-known prayer, which most older people will have learned at school, is the 'Our Father', or Lord's Prayer, which is a prayer Jesus taught his followers to say. Most Christian church services include this prayer. Prayers can be a deep source of comfort and reassurance when residents are going through difficult times, so it is good to note which prayers are meaningful. A prayer that is often quoted is the Serenity Prayer:

> God, give me the serenity to accept the things I cannot change;
> Courage to change the things I can;
> And wisdom to know the difference.

Anna Chaplains and others can often leave prayers on a card, leaflet, or bookmarker that can be gifted and kept by a resident if wanted. Appendix III (page 125) has other prayers that are commonly said by Christians.

The Bible

All the rituals and ceremonies in the Christian faith have their roots in the holy book of the faith, the Bible. The Bible has an Old Testament, which has books written before Jesus' time, including the Psalms, and a shorter New Testament written after Jesus was alive which chronicles his life and teachings. The Old Testament is the Jewish Torah, or holy book. Christians vary in how much they read the Bible, but some have a long-held practice of reading it every day.

Some Christian residents may be distressed if they do not have a Bible to read. An Anna Chaplain, minister, church member, or GOOD NEWS for Everyone! (**goodnewsuk.com**) can provide a copy of the Bible on request. The Bible is available in most languages spoken around the world, over 3,500 languages in total! Wycliffe Bible Translators has helpful information about where to find a Bible in a desired language (**wycliffe.org.uk**).

Fasting

Religious beliefs sometimes involve fasting or going without food and drink. For Muslims, Ramadan is a season of fasting. Christians also fast in certain traditions. This might be a simple change of diet for a season, such as Lent. Fasting goes hand in hand with prayer.

Rosaries and holding crosses

For some Christians, especially Catholics, a rosary (or prayer beads) is an aid to prayer. We have heard of care home residents who are distressed when they are parted from their rosary. As a symbol of the Christian faith, the cross is an important object. Some residents may find reassurance from keeping a holding cross in their hands, usually made of wood, but sometimes also knitted or made of fabric.

Sacraments

You may hear the word 'sacrament' used to describe key aspects of the Christian faith. A sacrament is a channel of God's grace brought about by Jesus Christ. The sacraments are an outward sign of inward grace where divine favour and spiritual assistance are to be found. Through the sacraments believers grow in the faith and in their relationship with God.

In the Catholic faith, for example, there are seven sacraments as signs of God's grace, several of which are held dear within other Christian denominations: baptism; confirmation; Holy Communion; confession; marriage; holy orders; anointing of the sick.

Baptism

A key principle of Christianity is baptism. The person who is being baptised is washed in water and sometimes anointed with oil. This symbolises being cleansed from sin and wrongdoing (anything that separates us from God), by God's grace, and rising forgiven from the water to a new life made possible by God the Son giving up his life to die a criminal's death to pay the price for the sins of the whole world.

Some Christian denominations baptise infants, but others wait until the person is an adult so they can have a 'believer's' baptism by 'full immersion' in a baptism pool or even a lake or river. Water holds symbolism in Christian faith; baptism in water reminds us that we have been forgiven through the death of Jesus. At services during the Christian calendar, Christians may be sprinkled with water to remind them of their baptism. Baptist churches are among those who hold to adult baptism.

Confirmation

For churches where infants are baptised, godparents and parents hold the faith of the child, promising to bring them up in the Christian faith until they are old enough to make their own commitment. This faith commitment is called confirmation. In the Church of England (or Anglican Church), people are confirmed by their bishop. They make promises to live by the Christian faith, and the bishop anoints them with oil on their forehead and prays for them. Before confirmation, candidates receive instruction in the Christian faith.

It is never too late to be baptised and confirmed. Some residents who have attended church services in their care home have come to faith, or returned to faith, and asked to be baptised and/or confirmed. This is arranged through an appropriate local church.

Other denominations have a variety of ways of recognising those who belong to the church. In the Methodist Church you are received into membership at a special service.

Holy Communion/Eucharist

Almost all Christian churches have Holy Communion, or Eucharist, as a regular part of their common life. The Salvation Army is one of the few churches that don't. Who has permission to take Communion, and the form it takes, can vary.

You may be aware of children taking their First Holy Communion. This is an important rite of passage in the Catholic Church and involves careful preparation and traditions, such as girls wearing white dresses. Taking Communion is associated with making a faith commitment and promises. By the time they are admitted to full-time care, some residents will have been receiving Communion every week since childhood. It imparts strength, comfort, and reassurance of the love of God, and a sense of belonging to a worldwide Christian family.

The origin of Holy Communion is found in the life of Jesus Christ. Just before he was arrested and killed by crucifixion, he told his followers to observe this 'meal' in remembrance of him. The Bible describes how over his final meal with them:

> Jesus took bread, and whn he had given thanks, he broke it and have it to his disciples, saying, 'Take and eat; this is my body.' Then he took a cup, and when he had given thanks, he gave it to them, saying, 'Drink from it, all of you. This is my blood of the covenant, which is poured out for many for the forgiveness of sins.'
> **MATTHEW 26:26–28**

The word 'Communion', therefore, refers to Christians sharing bread and wine to remember Jesus dying to rebuild the relationship between God and humankind that had been broken by our wrongdoing. There are special prayers said in receiving Communion, also known as a liturgy for Communion. For those who know nothing about this religious ritual, it might seem strange, but it is of profound significance to Christians and central to their faith. If they miss taking Communion for several months, this can be distressing.

Communion takes differing forms across the various Christian churches. In Methodist churches, there are individual miniature cups with non-alcoholic wine and you may be offered a small square of bread. In other churches, everyone drinks from the same cup, which is wiped with a cloth after each person has taken some wine. Some churches use a loaf of bread from which each person takes a chunk, but in other churches small round wafers are given. Sometimes the bread or wafer is eaten and then the wine or juice offered, but there is another practice where the bread or wafer is dipped in the wine or juice.

In many churches, there are restrictions over who can give Communion. In Anglican and Catholic churches, an ordained person must be the one to pray over the bread and wine and give the bread or wafer to each person. However, there is also the possibility of 'Sick Communion', or Home Communion, where permission is given for a member of the congregation to take the bread and wine the priest has consecrated to someone who cannot come to church. You may see an Anna Chaplain or other visitor from your local church bring residents Communion, which they give individually, perhaps in the person's room, or collectively in a service.

Obvious implications arise for the safety and well-being of residents in taking Communion. While there is great solace and peace to be found in this lifelong practice, for some people there are reasons why being given the bread, wafer, wine, or juice might be problematic. For some residents it may present a choking hazard. It is essential staff are involved and able to indicate where it is not advisable for an individual to be given the bread and wine. An alternative is for the person who brings the Communion to take them on behalf of the person; another is for the person to be offered an individual prayer of blessing instead.

The bread and wine hold symbolic significance for all communicants, but for those of the Catholic faith, through a doctrine called transubstantiation, they become Jesus' body and blood through the prayers said by the priest. If the bread or wafer falls on the floor, or the person receiving it is unable to swallow it and spits it out of their mouth, it is taken discretely and disposed of carefully.

Case study

Maria

Maria is a relatively new resident at Oaktree Lodge. She is clearly unsettled and her dementia makes it difficult to remember how she came to be living in the care home. At times she is agitated and restless, walking up and down the corridors seemingly looking for someone, especially in the afternoons. She can be heard to say under her breath, 'Oh God, Oh God, Oh God.'

Maria's friend Agnes visits regularly. She mentions that Maria was a regular churchgoer and that her faith is important to her. Amy, the well-being coordinator, makes a note of this and invites Maria to the next church service organised by the local parish church. Maria doesn't fully understand when Amy comes to bring her to the service but when she enters the lounge and hears the hymn being played as people arrive, there is a look of recognition on her face.

Amy observes Maria through the service. She notices how her facial expression and body language relax as the service begins. Maria joins in with the singing and seems to know the words. When it comes to the Communion towards the end of the service, Maria holds out her hands to receive the Communion wafer.

The sense of calm stays with Maria for the rest of the day, and she is less agitated through the evening than would often be the case.

Confession

A practice most associated with Catholicism is confession. If you have visited Catholic churches in this country or abroad, you will have noticed small confessional booths divided by a screen. The priest sits on one side of the screen and the penitent on the other side. The priest hears their confessions and offers absolution – or in other words, they tell the priest what they have done wrong, and the priest prays for their forgiveness. Some seasons of the year, such as Lent (the weeks before Easter) are known as penitential seasons. Friday is the day of the week associated with confession.

Even for those not in the Catholic tradition, the opportunity to talk about the things you regret as you are nearing the end of your life can be a great relief. Having someone who will listen and then pray for you as you confess to God the things you are sorry for is a way to find peace and reconciliation. Anna Chaplains 'hear' and give witness to some heartfelt conversations where residents retell part of their lives; this can feel like a kind of confession that can also bring peace.

Marriage

It is not unheard of for marriages to take place in care homes, and this is also a ceremony where local church leaders and chaplains may have a part to play, both in helping with preparation and on the day of the wedding itself. Sometimes staff members want to share their wedding with residents in the care home, and Anna Chaplains have been involved in blessing-of-marriage services after the event has taken place in another setting.

Beliefs about the afterlife, end-of-life prayers

Christians believe this world is not all there is. They believe when they die they will be in heaven, where they will see God face to face and be reunited with their loved ones. In heaven there will be no more crying or injustice. Death is not seen as the end, as it has been defeated by Jesus. In other faiths, beliefs about the afterlife include reincarnation, where we return in another form. What people believe about what happens after death shapes how they approach their own death and dying. For those whose belief is that there is nothing after death, attitudes and goals may differ from those who think there is something else.

Anointing the sick and praying for the dying

In some Christian traditions, prayers are said for a person who is sick while they are anointed with oil. This includes special prayers that are said with the dying person, sometimes called 'last rites'. This is true of other religions, too. There is great meaning and comfort in these prayers. They may be said by a priest but could also be said by another member of the Christian community. An Anna Chaplain, if you have one visiting, may be willing to sit with a resident who is dying and say prayers.

Residents in holy orders

Many clergy and ministers will end their days in a care home and may well want to share their faith in particular ways until the end. Others may have been in holy orders, living in religious communities as nuns or monks following a life set apart and dedicated to God. In dementia some may believe they are still in active ministry; and this abiding sense of purpose and identity can be respected and affirmed in the ways that enable them to express their calling and concern for other members of the community.

The role of faith leaders

Christians vary in their view of church leaders. Some have what you might call a 'high' view of the role of the church leader, others a 'low' view. For some residents it means a great deal to see the person with the dog collar, i.e. the priest, whereas for others being with fellow Christians no matter their role is the key. This can mean that residents might say no one from the church has visited them if the priest has not been to see them, even if members of their church visit regularly! Anna Chaplains are sometimes 'ordained' people who are priests and wear a dog collar, but more often they are what we call 'lay' people, who are not ordained.

In conclusion

The sacraments most likely to be practised by your Christian residents are Communion, confession in its various forms, and end-of-life religious care. As in all aspects of care, the wishes of the resident are central. Recording specific religious practices within the person's care plan is key in enabling their importance to be recognised by all members of staff. Residents of faiths other than Christianity will have their own rites and rituals, including at end of life, which play a crucial part in their well-being.

How to engage in spiritual conversations with individuals approaching end of life

Debbie Thrower

Care staff are at the forefront of helping people in this final part of their life's journey. You may feel responsible, yet in some cases poorly equipped, to offer spiritual care to the dying.

When it comes to looking after someone holistically at the end of their life, spiritual care – along with medical, practical, and emotional care – is an important part of the well-being of each individual resident.

Whether or not someone has been a churchgoer or has a professed faith, they would undoubtedly wish to be offered dignified and appropriate comfort when it comes to facing their own mortality.

This chapter aims to help you lend that support when you are the main person with whom they have contact at this highly significant point in their lives.

While it is a privilege to draw alongside the dying, it is not an easy path, and this chapter seeks to make it as fulfilling for you, and those you care for, as possible. Your role also includes enabling friends, family, and members of the wider community (including chaplains and visitors from the person's faith community) to be present at the end of life, supporting them in this.

When someone is fading

As the end of life draws near, it is natural to want to retreat from activity and to prefer a degree of peace and quiet. That doesn't mean a resident doesn't long for some human company, especially for someone who will listen to what they need and who will seek to answer their questions.

> A hospice patient was once asked, 'What do you need most?' He replied, 'For someone to look as if they are trying to understand me.'
>
> A patient's reply to Dame Cicely Saunders' question while he was being cared for at St Christopher's Hospice, south London

Some of life's biggest questions may trouble us as we realise that we are approaching death. Have I led a good life? What's going to happen to 'me' when I die? Are my loved ones going to be all right when I'm gone?

You can't expect to have ready-made answers or solutions to such questions, let alone have all the right words to hand to answer what is, after all, life's biggest mystery – what happens to us after death. But you can be a reassuring presence, offer a hand to hold, and give the dying person confidence that they will not suffer undue pain. You can assure the person who is dying that 'everything is going to be all right'.

The dying person is likely to become more and more sleepy, and times of sleep may become longer times of unconsciousness. You can continue to talk to them even when this is the case. Sitting in silence with them can also be a great comfort.

Reassuring phrases you can use include:

- 'God is watching over you.'
- 'You are in God's hands.'
- 'We all love you, but you can let go now.'
- 'Go in peace.'

Tell them why you think they are special, perhaps sharing your own happy memories of time spent with them. You can smile and even laugh as you voice these things.

If relatives of the dying person are not able to visit, perhaps you could suggest that they send in some short one-sentence memories of their loved one or a list of things they love about them. You can then read them to the resident (even if they are seemingly asleep or unconscious).

- ‘Maria remembers you teaching her how to knit teddy bears!’
- ‘Tom loves the way you’ve always cheered him up.’
- ‘Indira loves you very much.’

Doing this will also be helpful for the relatives who may be feeling helpless at home, not being able to visit. You could also ask them if they know of any favourite poems, hymns, or Bible readings that their loved one might like to hear.

A Covid survivor wrote an account of what got him through while he was in hospital. It seems that it was, to a large extent, good spiritual care:

> When you are as ill as I was, you return to a childlike state of total dependence on the kindness of others. I would not be here without the professionalism and dedication of the staff of the NHS. But my abiding memory of that time is of human kindness and compassion. A nurse bringing me a cup of tea in the middle of the night; giving me a shave on my birthday; whispering in my ear, ‘It’s going to be okay.’ In my hour of need, I reached out and found the hand of the NHS holding mine.
>
> Hylton Murray-Philipson, *The Spectator*, 18 April 2020

Case study

Olive

A former Macmillan nurse and nun, Sister Elizabeth Farmer, worked in Liverpool and was introduced to a woman called Olive.

Olive was dying of lung cancer. She lived alone, seemed to have no close friends or relatives, and refused to go to hospital. She was an atheist and at first unhappy to be visited by a nun. But Sister Elizabeth discovered that Olive had loved mountain climbing and won her trust by helping her to visualise her illness in the language of mountaineering.

When Olive's bed had to move to the ground floor because she could no longer manage the stairs, the nun called it 'base camp' and arranged for one wall to be covered in landscape photographs of mountains. Late one night, Olive phoned Sister Elizabeth and asked whether she could go into hospital for a couple of days.

Olive said to me, 'I'm glad I'm going in because I am going to do the most difficult climb of my life, but at the top I am going to see the most wonderful sunrise.' That's the nearest we got to God, but to me that was a totally spiritual saying. She died about three hours later.

From 'An ordered end', *Plus*, vol. 32, no. 4, Winter 2016. The quarterly magazine of Christians on Ageing.

How to pray with someone

To support someone spiritually is to offer friendship and companionship and (when possible and still appropriate) to facilitate access to those aspects of life that matter uniquely to them, which are very often linked to creativity. If music is comforting for them, for example, then a CD player or wireless speaker with their favourite types of music playing in the background might be much appreciated.

Depending on the person, this may also mean connecting, or reconnecting, someone with the religious faith traditions which have helped define who they are as an individual, and to pray with them. In the absence of someone from church (or other faith representative), that might mean you are the one they look to for that sort of comfort and reassurance.

So if this isn't your personal custom, how do you go about it? The Christian prayer that most people know from their childhood onwards is the Lord's Prayer, the one that Jesus taught his disciples to say when they asked him to teach them how to pray. It's amazing how often someone who appears to be asleep will stir and begin to join in when you say the words of the Lord's Prayer (see appendix III, page 125–26).

The resident might have enjoyed singing hymns, and the words of familiar ones might be well-known to them even as their life ebbs away. Try reading out the words of such hymns, such as the following from appendix I (page 109):

- 'What a friend we have in Jesus'
- 'Guide me, O thou great redeemer'
- 'Be thou my vision'

The book of Psalms in the Bible is also a rich source of prayers for those who are sick or distressed in any way, or who want some calming words to put them fully at their ease.

You might like to read portions of various psalms, such as Psalm 23 or 139 (see appendix II, page 115). These are often best remembered in their traditional forms.

As death draws near

Consider how the room might become a special place. Could you put some fresh flowers in there and perhaps an electric or battery-powered candle? Or place an object that was special to the person by their side – a Bible, a teddy bear, or a cross? Perhaps the family would have something to suggest?

These things, along with the quiet and dignified care that you are giving to the dying resident, will all help to create a sacred space that reflects this important journey to the end of someone's earthly life.

We know that hearing is often the last sense that we lose. Even when we may no longer see, we might hear what is going on around us.

When you sense that time is running out and the dying person may no longer be able to express their wishes (provided that you have established a good enough relationship), you will know whether they would welcome a prayer.

Here is a selection of short verses from scripture you might like to say. You could repeat them slowly and clearly:

> Whether we live or die, we belong to the Lord.
> ROMANS 14:8

> We will be with the Lord forever.
> 1 THESSALONIANS 4:17

> We shall see [God] as he is.
> 1 JOHN 3:2

> The Lord is my light and my salvation – whom shall I fear?
> PSALM 27:1

> I remain confident of this: I will see the goodness of the Lord in the land of the living. Wait for the Lord; be strong and take heart and wait for the Lord.
> PSALM 27:13–14

Into your hands I commit my spirit; deliver me, Lord, my faithful God.
PSALM 31:5

[Jesus says,] 'Truly I tell you, today you will be with me in paradise.'
LUKE 23:43

[Jesus says,] 'For my Father's will is that everyone who looks to the Son and believes in him shall have eternal life, and I will raise them up at the last day.'
JOHN 6:40

[Jesus says,] 'My Father's house has many rooms… I go and prepare a place for you, I will come back and take you to be with me that you also may be where I am.'
JOHN 14:2–3

[Jesus says,] 'Father, I want those you have given me to be with me where I am, and to see my glory, the glory you have given me because you loved me before the creation of the world.'
JOHN 17:24

'Lord Jesus, receive my spirit.'
ACTS 7:59

Because of the Lord's great love we are not consumed, for his compassions never fail. They are new every morning; great is your faithfulness.
LAMENTATIONS 3:22–23

We know that… we have a building from God, an eternal house in heaven, not built by human hands.
2 CORINTHIANS 5:1

These are just suggestions. Prayer can be as simple as you like. We are encouraged to pray as we can, not as we can't! Some of the most beautiful prayers I've ever heard are the ones children say, which come straight from the heart.

In the quiet, sitting with someone whose earthly life is drawing to a close, you might want to just give thanks for that person, name them before God, and wish them well on the next part of their journey.

It's been said that 'wasting time' with people is one of the most valuable things we ever do! Time spent accompanying someone as they die must surely be one of the very best uses of our time. Perhaps someone kind will do the same for us when our time comes?

> Looking back it will be the people we give thanks for... The great mystery and glory of the work is that we lead those people out of their physicality into the spiritual bodiliness of God's kingdom.
>
> David Scott, *Moments of Prayer* (SPCK, 1997)

In conclusion

Being with a dying person in the final moments of their life is a great privilege and a natural part of care home life. Creating a spiritually comforting environment through the physical environment of the person's room and the presence we bring is a wonderful gift that completes the person's time in the care home with dignity and respect.

In chapter 9 we will consider aspects of self-care for staff working in care homes. Support for staff when residents die is vital in acknowledging the toll bereavements can take in a setting where we make emotional connections with older people in our care. Valuing each older person who belongs to our care home community, even if only for a short period of time, means that losing them can hit hard.

How to have a memorial service when you are unable to attend the funeral

The Revd Sally Rees

This chapter is written to give you some ideas about how you might mark the passing of someone you cared for by taking some time to reflect on their memory and say goodbye. This is something you may wish to do yourself at home or something that you could do with a resident or group of residents in a care home. If you are holding such a thanksgiving or memorial service with residents in a care home, you will probably know what might work best for your needs and theirs. You can plan the short service together. It might be good for you to have your service on the same day as the funeral, but you can be flexible and choose a time that is suitable for you.

If it is a family member who is grieving and who would like to have a separate memorial service, this chapter shows them where to start, so please do share this chapter with them.

At a funeral, we are given the opportunity to set aside a specific time to remember the person we love, to say our own 'thank yous' for that person and to say our own goodbyes. A funeral may also be a time when we come before God with prayers, hymns, and readings, where the deceased has been a person of faith. We are acknowledging that the person is no longer with us and so, in Christian funerals, we also commit the person into God's loving care from this moment on.

Direct cremations have grown in popularity in recent years as a low-cost unattended alternative to a funeral service. Direct cremation may have been chosen by the person who has died as a way of minimising cost and effort, but the opportunity a funeral gives for bereaved relatives and friends to celebrate their life and come together in mourning their loss is not then available. A memorial service as described here provides a way of marking a loved one's passing and drawing strength from being together. Churches are also willing to hold a service of thanksgiving in their church buildings for those who have opted for direct cremation so that the bereaved can gather and remember the person who has died.

What does a memorial service look like?

A memorial service can take any form you want. There are many elements to a funeral service, but a memorial service can have just one or two elements. Its main purpose is to give you a time to remember that person and to mark their passing.

Elements of a funeral service that you might choose to include for a memorial are, for example:

- Creating a quiet space and starting the service
- Lighting a candle
- Reflecting on the person's life
- Hymns
- Bible readings
- Prayers
- Saying goodbye
- Ending the memorial time together

For your memorial service at home, use any of these elements that you find helpful. The service can be as short or as long as you wish.

Creating a quiet space and starting the service

You might like to set up a small table with a pretty cloth, a small vase of flowers, and a photograph or object that will remind you of the loved one, as a focal point for your service.

You might like to start the service with a simple sentence, such as: 'We meet in this act of love and respect to honour our loved one *[insert name]*, who has died.'

Lighting a candle

Light a candle or an electric tea-light and take some time (the length of time is entirely up to you) to think about the person who has died and all that they meant to you. The candle can also be a reminder that Jesus, the light of the world, is there with you.

Reflecting on the person's life

At a funeral, there is normally a spoken eulogy or tribute to the person, remembering some of the details of their unique life. At a service at home, this is not so easy and may be too formal, but there are other ways that you can evoke cherished memories. If you want to, choose one or more that works for you:

- Focus on a photograph or hold something in your hand that reminds you of them. Write a list of what you liked about the person – why they were special to you.
- Either in silence or out loud, bring your memories of the person to mind (or in prayer). This can be as formal or as informal as you wish and can take as long as you want.

Play a piece of music that they liked, and use the time that the track is playing to have your own thoughts and prayers.

Read a poem or a piece of prose that reflects how you feel about the person.

This might be all that you need to remember and honour the person who has died. If you want to put more of a 'service' together, some other suggestions follow.

Hymns

At a funeral, you would normally sing at least two hymns. Unless you are a confident singer, you might prefer not to do this. Alternatively, you could listen to a hymn or two, using a CD player if available (you can find a suitable resource in appendix I, page 109) or, if you have access to the internet, you could find the hymn online. Here are some common hymns that people choose:

- 'Abide with me'
- 'Amazing grace'
- 'Guide me, O thou great redeemer'
- 'The day thou gavest, Lord, is ended'
- 'The old rugged cross'
- 'The Lord's my shepherd'

There are many other beautiful hymns, and the choice is entirely yours.

Bible readings

In a Christian funeral, there are one or more Bible readings that are an integral part of the service. There are some wonderful Bible readings that are appropriate to read at this time. The types of reading fall into a few categories. These are:

- Very comforting readings, including many of the psalms, such as Psalm 23 or 121.
- More matter-of-fact readings, such as Ecclesiastes 3:1 – 'There is a time for everything, and a season for every activity under the heavens.'
- Readings about a God-given characteristic, such as 1 Corinthians 13, which is all about love.

- Readings about what Jesus told his disciples concerning life after death, such as John 14:1–7.
- Pictures of heaven, like the one in Revelation 21:1–5.

This sample of Bible readings can be found in appendix II, page 115.

Prayers

At a Christian funeral, there would normally be three types of prayers: first, to thank God for the person who has died; second, to pray for those who mourn; and, third, a prayer that looks forward, reminding us that death is not the end. We can be hopeful because we have the promise of eternal life with Jesus in God's presence.

These can be very simple, for example:

- Father God, thank you for our loved one *[insert name]* and for all that they meant to us. Thank you for the lovely memories that we shared. Help us to cherish them always.
- Father God, comfort those who mourn, especially *[insert names]*. Be very close to them today and in the coming weeks and months and give them your peace.
- Father God, as we think of the future, help us to give our loved one *[insert name]* to you, knowing that they are in your safe keeping.

Funerals usually involve saying the Lord's Prayer (see appendix III, page 125–26) together, so if you would like to pray just one prayer, do pray this one.

Saying goodbye

You can just say your own farewells, but there is a prayer from the Bible that is sometimes said at the end of a funeral service, if you would like to use it. It is called the Nunc Dimittis and is part of the evening prayer service of the Anglican Church:

Lord, now lettest thou thy servant depart in peace: according to thy word. For mine eyes have seen: thy salvation; which thou hast prepared: before the face of all people; to be a light to lighten the Gentiles: and to be the glory of thy people Israel.

Glory to the Father, and to the Son, and to the Holy Ghost; as it was in the beginning, is now, and ever shall be: world without end. Amen.

Ending the memorial time together

The Nunc Dimittis is a wonderful ending to the service. However, there are other ways of appropriately closing such a service. Two suggestions are:

- Say the Grace:

  May the grace of the Lord Jesus Christ, and the love of God, and the fellowship of the Holy Spirit be with you all. Amen.

- Say a blessing. There are lots that you can yse. You can simply say, 'Peace be with you.' Or use this Celtic blessing:

  May the road rise up to meet you. May the wind be always at your back. May the sunshine be warm upon your face; the rains fall soft upon your fields and, until we meet again, may God hold you in the palm of his hand.

Finally

If you would like a simple prepared service, there is an example in appendix VI (page 149). There are also resources and advice available on the Church of England website (**churchofengland.org/life-events/funerals**), including 'Support for when you can't attend a funeral'.

Resources

The day of the funeral or the memorial service is just the first milestone on the bereavement journey. It is an important ritual to slowly ease the grief of losing someone we have been close to. There are many resources that may help as time goes on. Below are a few suggestions.

The Path Not Chosen: Beginning the journey of loss and bereavement by Wendy Bray has a one-step-at-a-time approach to grieving. It is a 16-page booklet published by Waverley Abbey Trust in 2021 and available through online bookshops at around £2 per copy.

Praying Our Goodbyes: A spiritual companion through life's losses and sorrows by Joyce Rupp has prayers to help and give comfort through many of life's losses. It was published by Ave Maria Press in 2009 and is available through online bookshops.

If you have internet access, At a Loss (**ataloss.org**) is a UK signposting website for directing the bereaved and those supporting them to information and services appropriate to their loss; promoting and encouraging the bereavement support that exists; plugging gaps in bereavement support where it is scarce; and training groups and individuals in bereavement care to mobilise local support. The organisation also has an online chat site for those who are grieving. It also has details of a seven-week course (weekly, for two hours at a set date and time) called 'The Bereavement Journey'.

Please also speak to your Anna Chaplain, priest, minister, or pastoral visitor, who may be able to support you or will find the right person to 'walk with you' during this time of loss and adjustment.

Postscript

How the news of a death is conveyed to other residents is a sensitive area and one where your local churches and Anna Chaplains might offer support. It is sometimes felt that residents should not be told when someone has died, for fear of upsetting them. However, this can lead to confusion and questions over what has happened to the person. Care homes have found respectful ways to mark a resident's passing which convey the news with dignity. Passing on the news gently in individual conversation with residents who have been close to the person, and offering support, helps ease the uncertainty and provides a context for grief.

Some churches hold a special annual memorial service. This may be around All Souls' Day (late October/early November), around the time of Remembrance Day (November), or at Easter. The names of those who have died may be read out and opportunity given for friends and family to remember and give thanks. Churches and Anna Chaplains often work with the care homes they visit to provide a memorial service for residents and staff to remember those in their community who have died.

In conclusion

Supporting one another through the loss of a person who has been a part of our life is essential for everyone in a care home community – residents, visitors, and staff. Ways of celebrating and remembering the life of someone who has died enable collective grief and show that that person was an important member of the care home family.

Faith groups and chaplains can be helpful collaborators in putting in place appropriate services and rituals for mourning our losses.

Case study

Mavis

Mavis often spoke with staff at Lakeview about her dear friend Ethel. The two had grown up together and been lifelong companions. The love and joy on Mavis' face when she talked about Ethel were plain for all to see. Mavis had never married and staff sometimes wondered if her bond with Ethel was more than just platonic.

As they both became frail in later life, their wider families took decisions out of their hands and they were placed in different care homes, unable to see each other. Activity organiser James introduced Mavis to Skype and worked with Ethel's home to enable them to talk regularly. Mavis was so grateful, and her conversations with Ethel were the highlight of her weeks, even if she was sometimes tearful afterwards, clearly missing having her dear friend close by.

When news came through to the home that Ethel had died, staff working with Mavis knew how devastated she would be. Given her own fragile state of health, it was impossible for her to attend the funeral. So James worked with colleagues to create a memorial service for Ethel on the same day as the funeral.

The service was held in the quiet room at Lakeview, and Mavis' niece Alice came. A photograph of Ethel was placed on the table alongside an LED candle and a vase of yellow roses (Ethel's favourite flower). Mavis chose Ethel's favourite pieces of music to be played during the service, and there was a time of sharing stories from the many happy times they spent together. Tears were shed, and the pain of loss remained intense for Mavis, but she felt she had been able to say goodbye to Ethel and celebrate her life.

Creative approaches

Julia Burton-Jones

This chapter introduces a range of activities and resources aimed at celebrating residents' spiritual and religious identities and enabling them to express their beliefs, values, and cultures. Spiritual and religious life is far broader than taking part in a church service, reading religious materials, or praying regularly.

Sharing our perspectives on life and having opportunities to learn how others see the world is interesting, life affirming, and mind-broadening; older people don't lose that curiosity. Several of the suggestions below are simple and low-cost; others require some investment in resources and craft materials.

Discussion groups

Spiritual and religious topics can spark meaningful conversation and enable a group of residents to make connections and get to know one another better. It could be as simple as introducing a question or topic linked to beliefs, values, traditions, or wisdom received via older relatives.

Proverbs and sayings

Proverbs used in everyday life often say something important about values and beliefs:

- Let sleeping dogs lie
- The grass is always greener on the other side
- There's no place like home
- A leopard can't change its spots

Books of proverbs and sayings are readily available at relatively low cost, some with proverbs familiar to those who have lived in the UK, but others drawing from cultures across the world. Though now out of print, you can still purchase on used-book websites a lovely 'Pictures to Share' large hardback illustrated book called *Proverbs and Sayings* by Helen Bate (Pictures to Share Community Interest Company, 2013). 'Pictures to Share' books are designed to spark conversation with people with dementia through the use of attractive images and text in large font. Many websites feature proverbs, too.

You could ask residents to finish a proverb after quoting the first phrase. You could discuss what the proverb or saying means and where it comes from. Ask if residents agree with the sentiment expressed and if it has proven true in their lives.

Conversation games

There are many resources designed to spark conversation which might be helpful in enabling discussions between residents. Anna Chaplaincy was involved in the creation of a conversation game called Table Talk for Fourth Agers produced by The Ugly Duckling Charity (**table-talk.org/fourth-agers**). It has questions aimed at fourth-agers under several headings: trivia; celebrating; relationships; memories; health; big issues. Under 'memories', for instance, there is a card with the question: 'What is the most precious photo that you own?'

Bible studies

A study group for residents who have been church members and perhaps part of a small Bible study group can be a good way to enable a sense of community and continuing growth and development in faith. There are many resources available for groups to use to study the Bible together, and there are many videos online aimed at enabling reflection on Bible passages. BRF Ministries is a good source of material (see appendix II, page 124, for some examples).

Studying other faiths

Learning about the faith and culture of others in the community – including residents and staff members – might be a helpful way to build connections and aid understanding.

Spiritual reminiscence

Elizabeth MacKinlay has written extensively about the spirituality of later life and dementia. She developed an approach to helping people living with dementia explore and share their spirituality, which she calls spiritual reminiscence. She suggests facilitating small group sessions to explore relevant topics, with a structure that might be as follows:

- Week 1: Life-meaning
- Week 2: Relationships/isolation/connecting
- Week 3: Hopes, fears and worries
- Week 4: Growing older and transcendence
- Week 5: Spiritual and religious beliefs
- Week 6: Spiritual and religious practices

In her book on facilitating spiritual reminiscence (Elizabeth MacKinlay and Corinne Trevitt, *Facilitating Spiritual Reminiscence for People with Dementia: A learning guide*, Jessica Kingsley, 2015), she provides material for these sessions and suggests they could be run in a care home setting.

Music and dance

Playlist for life

Enabling residents to enjoy personalised music is a valuable way to meet spiritual needs. Music is important to identity and helps define our story. Playlist for Life (**playlistforlife.org.uk**) is an organisation that gives wonderful guidance on creating playlists that are personally meaningful for people with dementia. They have guidance on creating a playlist and downloadable conversation starters and leaflets. You can encourage relatives and friends to help create a person's playlist.

BBC Music Memories

The BBC has a website called Music Memories (**musicmemories.bbcrewind.co.uk**) where you can listen to classical music, popular music over the decades, theme tunes, UK nations music, and international music. You can also tune in to Memory Radio, with music-based radio programmes accompanied by printable activity sheets with discussion questions linked to the music played in the show.

Music for Dementia

Music for Dementia (**musicfordementia.org.uk**) has M4D Radio, which has mixes for the 1940s, 1950s, 1960s, 1970s, and 1980s. It has many ideas and resources for musical activities, as well as information on the science of why music is such an effective tool for connecting with people with dementia.

Music Helps

Music Helps (**musichelps.training**) has free online courses to help carers use music to enable well-being in dementia, where music therapists offer guidance.

Live music

Sharing an experience of hearing music live is context for profound connections with others. Yehudi Menui, the co-founder of Live Music Now, said: 'Music… is the language which penetrates most deeply into the human spirit…' He was inspired to take professional musicians into care homes, hospitals, and hospices, among other places. Live Music Now (**livemusicnow.org.uk**) holds participatory concerts and enables musicians to have residences in care homes.

You may have local choirs, soloists, and ensembles willing to visit your home. Your local church choir, organist, or music group could get involved. You may have local schools willing to arrange for pupils to bring music into the home.

Circle dance

Expressing yourself through movement to music can provide wonderful release for those who struggle to communicate verbally. For many residents, dance has been a lifelong interest and source of connection and enjoyment.

Circle Dance for People Living with Dementia (**dementiapathfinders.org/circle-dance**) has been developed over many years in the UK from traditional folk dance from across the world. Music and dances have been simplified and adapted from traditional dances so that they can be seated and standing. Touch, holding, swaying, and simple repetitive movements allow the participant to feel safe within the circle, providing an opportunity for creativity and expression. It brings a sense of identity and belonging, and in so doing, meets spiritual needs. Circle Dance for People Living with Dementia is an activity offered in some care homes with staff trained by Dementia Pathfinders.

Other forms of dance have been adapted for use in dementia care settings. The English National Ballet, for example, has a Dance for Dementia programme. Explore sources of dance and movement in your local community.

Visual arts, creativity, and reminiscence

Craft activities

Creativity is closely linked with spirituality. Expressing ourselves by making something with colour, shape, and texture gives a sense of achievement and helps us show something of our inner selves.

For residents who have always enjoyed crafting and art, being enabled to continue in this, perhaps adapting the activity to account for altered abilities, enables the sense of self to be reinforced. We may find objects the person has created earlier in life displayed in their room, and inviting them to share the story of that artwork is an opportunity to discover what this creative endeavour means to them.

Some residents may not have considered themselves very creative but might be encouraged to have a go and find a new outlet for self-expression. Even simple colouring with age-appropriate resources can be therapeutic and provide a sense of satisfaction.

Loaning resources from museums or looking at collections online

Looking at works of art can also be a spiritual experience. If visits to local art galleries and museums is challenging, why not consider bringing works of art into the home, either through visiting online collections or by linking with the local library or museum to supply themed boxes of reminiscence objects?

Storytelling and intergenerational activities

Bible storytelling

A care home in Kent invited their Anna Chaplain to visit and simply read Bible stories with residents. She used a youth version of the Bible that had helpful explanations of the context of the story. The Old Testament book of Ruth was a particular favourite.

Messy Vintage

Messy Vintage (**messychurch.brf.org.uk/messy-vintage**) is a BRF Ministries initiative linked to Messy Church and Anna Chaplaincy. Messy Church is an intergenerational form of church which is relaxed, informal, and creative. When held in the community it would often be on a Sunday afternoon and typically once a month, attracting families and individuals who may not feel comfortable in a more traditional Sunday morning service. You might have three-generational family groups – children with their parents and grandparents. Based on a Bible passage, it includes elements of crafting, singing, storytelling, and sharing food together which bring a sense of belonging, fun, and community.

Messy Vintage takes the principles of Messy Church and applies them to events aimed at older people and held in a church building or a care home. Many Anna Chaplains offer Messy Vintage as part of what they can provide in the care homes they support. Sometimes the name is slightly different (e.g. Vintage Adventure) but the focus is craft activity illustrating the theme, plus discussing, singing, and praying together. Reminiscence is a key element of Messy Vintage. A useful resource is Katie Norman and Jill Phipps, *Messy Vintage: 52 sessions to share Christ-centred fun and fellowship with the older generation* (BRF Ministries, 2021).

OutoftheBox

OutoftheBox (**outofthebox.org**) is a way of using stories and play to facilitate a search for well-being and wisdom for people of all ages.

It is an approach used by chaplains in care homes across the world to bring spiritual care to older people. Stories draw on wisdom from myths, legends, traditional tales, children's literature, and various faith traditions. They are carefully scripted to enable those taking part to interpret and listen with the heart, exploring what they might mean through playful dialogue.

Each story has a box of storytelling materials often made from wood and fabric. While the story is being told, these items are placed before the group. The pacing of the story allows moments of quietness and invitations to ponder through the phrase, 'I wonder'. Chaplains have discovered that OutoftheBox enables older people, including those living with dementia, to have a greater sense of belonging in their community.

Truth Be Told

Truth Be Told (**truthbetold.org.uk**) is a Christian organisation that has developed a creative approach to intergenerational storytelling designed to give a sense of joy and belonging, especially to those at the edges of groups. It is used in many contexts, including schools, refuges for women and children, and migrant and refugee communities where members are learning English.

Truth Be Told is an excellent tool for engaging preschool children and residents in the care homes to which they are linked. Christian stories are told in simple and creative ways, and singing is an integral part of what happens each time. Sessions always begin with, 'Let me tell you a story...' Sessions end with a key affirming message, such as 'You are loved' or 'You are heard'.

Links with local schools, groups for preschool children, and uniformed organisations

Linking with a local preschool, primary, or secondary school is an excellent way to bring children and young people into a care home. Chaplains and church visitors may be people who can help forge these links, especially with faith-based schools. Often visits are linked to seasons in the calendar, such as holding carol services or performances at Christmas. Anna Chaplaincy has a two-page downloadable Easy Guide with examples and suggestions – 'Easy Guide 2: Linking care homes with local schools' (**annachaplaincy.org.uk/easy-and-church-guides**).

Churches often host or run 'toddler groups', which are drop-in community sessions for parents, grandparents, and carers to bring babies and preschool children for a time of play. Some Anna Chaplains have invited parents and carers who attend their toddler group to visit the care home with their children for a time of creativity, singing, or storytelling.

Children and young people are also involved in uniformed groups linked with churches (e.g. Beavers, Cubs, Scouts, Rainbows, Brownies, Guides, Girls' Brigade, Boys' Brigade). You may have members of staff or volunteers with links to these groups.

Visiting animals

Pets as Therapy (PAT)

For many residents, pets have been a great source of companionship and meaning in life. If they have given up a much-loved pet to come into the care home, this in itself entails a process of mourning. Treasured memories of long-lost pets are a great conversation starter, a way to help a new resident open up about themselves.

Spending time with well-trained animals can be a source of comfort and has been known to enable communication in cases where people have become cut off from those around them. Pets as Therapy or PAT (**petsastherapy.org**) is a network of volunteers willing to take their cat or dog into a care home, as well as other places like hospitals and schools. Volunteers are assessed by a PAT assessor and complete online safeguarding training.

Studies show that interacting with a PAT pet can boost mental health and overall well-being, bring moments of energy and joy for people with dementia, and strengthen bonds with carers and family. Some Anna Chaplains take their PAT dog with them on visits to their local care home.

Case study

Ulrika

Ulrika had been living at Yew Tree Lodge for over a year and had been admitted following a series of events in which she had been found a long way from home after her neighbour Joan had reported her missing. Her dementia had advanced fairly rapidly, and the care staff who looked after her were sad to see her retreat into her own world. She now said very little to them and would walk restlessly around the ground floor of the home as if searching for something or someone. Attempts to break through the invisible wall surrounding her were having mixed success, and staff felt they were losing her.

On a windy Wednesday morning, a new visitor arrived at Yew Tree Lodge: Jess the golden retriever with her Pets as Therapy volunteer owner Jason. Jess was gentle and allowed residents to stroke her as she made her way around the ground floor. Suddenly, Ulrika stopped in her tracks as she walked down the corridor for the umpteenth time. She had spotted Jess and changed course to enter the lounge where Jason and Jess were sitting. Taking a seat, she reached out to pat Jess who responded by coming closer. For the first time in weeks, staff were amazed to hear Ulrika speaking fluently to Jess. Her face looked animated, like the old Ulrika.

When her neighbour Joan next visited, staff asked her if she knew anything about Ulrika's past relationships with dogs. Joan said that Ulrika had owned many dogs over the years and had been a volunteer foster carer for abandoned dogs with the local animal shelter. She reminisced about Ulrika nursing sick and abandoned dogs back to health.

Now when Jess and Jason visit, they always spend time with Ulrika. Wednesdays are good days for her – seeing Jess lifts her spirits, and she is more communicative after the time spent with her, and visibly happier.

Other ways to enable residents to have contact with animals

Some care homes have their own resident pets or allow residents to bring an animal with them when they are admitted. You may have local organisations that arrange for animals to visit care homes as an activity. Or you could arrange a visit to a local wildlife sanctuary. The care home garden can be a place where residents can watch birds and wild animals, especially where birdfeeders are well placed to allow observation. Some residents will have worked with animals, perhaps in farming or veterinary care. Others will have been keen birdwatchers or nature lovers, enjoyed fishing, or even been on safari; looking at photos and encouraging sharing of memories taps into these interests in ways that are good for the soul.

Being mindful of those who are less happy with animals

Of course, there will be some for whom animals hold less happy feelings and memories, and this needs to be well understood and documented so that they are not distressed by visiting animals. Some may even have phobias over certain birds and animals. We may need to be aware of what animals signify in different faiths and cultures. Some animals hold sacred significance (such as cows in Hinduism), whereas others may be considered unclean (pigs in Judaism and Islam). In some interpretations of Islamic law, keeping dogs as pets is discouraged as being ritually impure, but cats are permissible.

Events and celebrations

Celebrating important times of the year for residents and staff of different faith and cultural groups is enriching for everyone. The Christian calendar governs many seasonal festivities, especially Easter and Christmas, but marking occasions important in other cultures honours the customs, beliefs, and values of a diverse community. Involving staff members, residents, and visitors in planning these special events linked to their cultural identity helps build a sense of belonging and connection.

Case study

Celebrating Caribbean culture

Sara worked as activity coordinator at Maple Court. One of her jobs was to organise a calendar of parties and celebrations, often inviting people from the local community to join in with the events.

Aware that several residents and staff members had Caribbean heritage, she consulted everyone about the possibility of holding a mini Carnival in late August, to coincide with the Notting Hill Carnival. This idea was received positively by residents and staff alike, and a date was put in the calendar.

Chef Anthony agreed to prepare some traditional Caribbean dishes, and a generous son of one of the residents offered to supply ingredients for rum punch! In the weeks leading up to the carnival, residents were involved in creating decorations for the home. Staff members agreed to dress up in Caribbean attire on the day, and a local steel band agreed to visit. Everyone was involved in choosing playlists for the day with, of course, an emphasis on Reggae music.

Sara was thrilled with how the celebrations went. There was a great party atmosphere on the Saturday of the event, with lots of friends and family members joining in. The weather was fantastic, so everyone felt able to spill out into the garden for the festivities. It was brilliant that residents and staff with Caribbean heritage felt able to share their stories and talk about the cultural treasures that meant so much to them.

Offering spaces for quiet reflection

In the same way hospitals and hospices have chapels where patients, staff, and visitors can spend time in quiet thought or prayer, care homes may also dedicate rooms or spaces for quiet reflection. These are sometimes called multifaith rooms or quiet rooms. They might hold religious objects and images, books of poetry, LED candles, and Bluetooth speakers to enable music to be played – or they might be quite plain and restful with no specific religious focus. When planning such a room, consult with residents, staff, and visitors to find out what would best serve their needs. These spaces can provide a restful place for visitors to spend time with a resident.

The care home garden can also provide a space for peaceful meditation and spiritual refreshment. A sensory garden with well-placed seating is a good place for contemplating and connecting with nature.

In conclusion

This chapter has hopefully illustrated that much of what is already happening in your care home has a spiritual dimension. Spiritual and religious care provision is about much more than a monthly church service or arranging for prayers to be said with a resident who is dying. Spiritual flourishing can encompass a wide range of activities that enable the person to express who they are and connect with others and the world around them.

Working effectively with local churches

Julia Burton-Jones

The aim of this chapter is to increase understanding of how care homes can work with churches of all denominations to enrich residents' lives. We will look at how churches and care homes can work together in a broad sense, not simply through responding to individual religious need. We will also think about how churches might have different denominational identities – Anglican, Catholic, Methodist, etc. – and what this signifies.

Working effectively with your local churches

You will be aware of a number of churches close to your care home, but you may not have considered how you might work with them, both as providers of religious and spiritual care and as community partners, enabling residents to make connections with the world beyond the care home.

Churches helping meet religious needs

It goes without saying that churches exist to meet religious and spiritual needs. While they may primarily focus on the spirituality of members, most also feel a responsibility to their community, including vulnerable older people and those living in care homes. They seek to express care and concern for frail older people living close to where they are based. They may pray regularly for local care homes, and members may have personal connections with residents and staff.

Sometimes care homes struggle to make a connection with a local church, such as not knowing who to contact or not receiving a response to messages left. Hopefully this is a minority experience. What might a care home ask and expect from a local church by way of support for its residents (and staff)?

As a minimum, you should expect the church to support residents who have been members there. This might be through a church minister bringing a short Communion service (see chapter 4), it might include members of the pastoral care team visiting, or it might simply be long-standing friends from the church popping in. These individuals can be like members of a second family for the resident; they know them well, and their visits can help someone settle in the home when they are feeling disorientated.

We would hope that the local church would be keen to support all residents in the home, including those with no previous links. Church visitors may be willing to spend time with people who have been regular churchgoers, both by befriending and praying with them individually, but also by holding regular church services at which anyone who wishes to come is welcome.

Naturally, care home managers and activities staff are concerned that those visiting the home understand and are sensitive to the needs of the care home population and that volunteers in churches who visit as part of the pastoral care team have been safely recruited, with the necessary training and DBS checks or equivalent to work with vulnerable adults. This is also true of chaplains like Anna Chaplains. Ask the church to provide this evidence for people they send in an official capacity and ensure they meet your own volunteer guidelines.

Where the local church is happy to provide a regular church service in your care home, this will have a similar structure to what might happen on a Sunday in church (with songs, prayers, Bible readings, and a reflection), but it will need to be responsive to the people who attend. You can work with the church volunteers to ensure the service is appropriate.

Over time, the church team will learn about the preferences and backgrounds of your residents and adapt the service to include favourite hymns and prayers and by asking residents if they want to contribute (e.g. by doing a Bible reading or making suggestions for prayers). You may have residents who have been in leadership roles in churches, and finding an outlet for them to continue fulfilling this sense of identity is helpful.

Another aspect of religious care your local church might provide is visiting residents individually to talk, pray, and read the Bible with them. This is especially important for residents who are confined to their rooms or who, for whatever reason, are unable to join a group for the regular service. They may also be willing to visit at short notice to pray with a resident who is very unwell or dying; you may receive a request for this from the resident, a close friend, or relative.

Case study

Eric

Eric was admitted to The Red House from hospital, initially as a short-term placement, though it was looking likely he would be staying permanently. The Red House was in a town several miles from where he had lived before. It was taking time for him to settle, and he was reluctant to join in with group activities in the home.

One day a team from the local church came for the regular services they held at The Red House, which included Holy Communion. Eric overheard them inviting other residents to join them. He attracted the attention of one of the visitors and asked if he might come, too, saying he had not realised that the church offered this. The visitor welcomed Eric to come with her, and as they were walking into the lounge where the service was to be held, he confided to her that he had been missing his own church very much and had been longing to take Communion since being in hospital.

Eric readily joined in with the prayers and hymns, and the church team were moved to see him shed tears of relief at receiving Communion. They spent time after the service chatting with him and promised to include him in future services. Staff noticed Eric's mood improve noticeably after taking part in the service of worship. It was the start of him being willing to participate in other regular groups and activities. His care plan was updated to reflect his Christian faith, and his keyworker checked to make sure he had a Bible he could read in his room.

Churches responding to wider spiritual needs

If an Anna Chaplain or other local church visitor forms a pattern of visiting your care home, they may ask how they can support residents who don't have a church background. They are concerned about the spiritual well-being of all your residents, whatever their beliefs or values. In this they are not seeking to force their faith on residents, from which you would rightly want to shield everyone.

Person-centred spiritual care starts from where the person is in their life and responds to them in the moment. It gives space for the person to talk about what matters to them, what brings them meaning and purpose, and any questions or concerns that are troubling them, without making assumptions or carrying expectations. Anna Chaplains and other church visitors may be willing to befriend residents who lack regular visitors and are isolated.

Some churches find that offering a regular activity, such as a craft or reminiscence group, is a brilliant way to get to know residents and provide a context where they are able to talk about what matters to them. A pattern might be for the team to visit monthly for a church service and then at another time to run an activity or speak with residents individually.

Churches enabling community engagement

Churches are part of your local community. They are made up of people who live in the neighbourhood and have links into other organisations. They can therefore be a means through which you can link residents with their community and enable them to enjoy a life outside the confines of the care home building. Clearly, they might want to go out to Sunday services, if they are able, but the church may also offer a welcome to midweek events, such as coffee mornings or singing groups. This provides a manageable low-cost outing and the opportunity to make connections with new friends.

Churches may also have links with groups for children and young people. They may host 'toddler groups' for preschool children and their parents and carers. They may have uniformed organisations (Cubs, Brownies, Guides, and Scouts) and a church school. This might enable wonderful intergenerational connections for your residents, with groups visiting to perform, perhaps, or to enjoy a seasonal party, or simply to talk or read with residents.

Establishing good working relationships with churches

Once you have made a positive connection with a local church and explored how they might work with the care home, it is best practice to create a shared agreement signed by representatives of the home and the church which gives a structure for this new working relationship. The agreement can then be reviewed regularly and updated to reflect changing circumstances. Appendix VIII (page 162) has a sample working agreement you could adapt. The agreement might include details of:

- Who will be visiting from the church and which member of staff they will liaise with in planning visits
- When visits will take place
- Regular church services that will be offered in the care home

- Individual support available from the church for residents as needed
- Expectations on both sides
- How church visitors will report to staff, particularly over safeguarding concerns
- A date for the agreement to be reviewed

The church or Anna Chaplain might provide a leaflet or poster enabling staff to inform residents and visitors of the service provided. This could be displayed on noticeboards in the home and will be evidence of spiritual and religious care for regulatory purposes.

Church visitors must be accompanied by staff. They cannot provide personal care and have limited knowledge of the care needs of individual residents. It is not appropriate to leave a group of residents with church volunteers while they are holding a church service in a lounge; staff may need to respond to care needs during the service. If the visitor is spending time in a resident's room, the door should be left open and staff members made aware the visit is happening so they can discretely observe the visit and respond if a need arises.

You may have a policy for volunteering in your care home which applies to visitors from local churches. A form of 'induction' is very helpful in enabling volunteers to navigate the building, understand the staffing structure, and gain a sense of the culture of care you are providing. Visitors need to be aware of measures you have in place to keep everyone safe, understanding the need to sign in and to liaise with members of staff during visits.

You may need to explain to church visitors that you cannot share a resident's personal information without that resident's permission. Staff can enable positive initial connections to be made so that residents sense the visitor is trustworthy; they may then feel comfortable over time in sharing aspects of their lives and spiritual identity. It may be that a resident discloses information to the visitor that sheds light on how they see the world. If the visitor feels this information will enable person-centred care, they might ask the resident's permission to tell the care home staff, so that this information can be added to the care plan. Safeguarding training received by church volunteers will impress upon them the need to alert senior staff immediately where disclosures of abuse are made in conversation with a resident.

As with all areas of activity, it will help you in evidencing spiritual care if you record visits by the local church or Anna Chaplain in the resident's daily care notes. In one Kent care home the manager developed a form that could be completed by the Anna Chaplain after each visit, listing residents with whom she had engaged and the themes of some of her conversations with them. These forms are kept securely in the office and relevant details added to individual care plans.

It may also be appropriate, particularly for residents with dementia, to inform next of kin of the involvement of the local church in their resident's life in the home. For some relatives, this will be reassuring, though for others faith may not be shared with the older person and the links may be seen as less relevant. If a person acting as next of kin is opposed to a resident having contact with the church, for whatever reason, a best interests judgement might be needed in understanding the resident's previous way of life and what their wishes would have been. Friends from church sometimes advocate on behalf of a resident whose family do not recognise the importance of faith.

Understanding different denominations in Christianity

The Christian faith is a worldwide religion dating back two millennia. The way it is practised has evolved to reflect culture and context, and this has led to groups branching off from the established church of their day to form new 'denominations'. These denominations hold to the same core Christian beliefs (also known as the Creed) but have their own traditions and ways of expressing them that reflect how they were established and their priorities and styles of worshipping.

This section is not offering a detailed description of each denomination but seeks to outline some distinctive characteristics. In explaining the rich history of the Christian community, the overarching aim is to demonstrate that a care home might want to foster links with several churches rather than seeing strong links with just one church as sufficient. A resident who has been a lifelong Methodist, for example, may request links to the local Methodist church even where the Church of England parish has a regular presence in the care home.

Major Christian denominations

The oldest Christian church in the UK is the Roman Catholic Church. The Anglican Church (Church of England, Church in Wales, Episcopalian Church in Scotland) broke away from the Catholic Church under the reign of King Henry VIII in the 16th century. The Anglican Church is called a 'Protestant' church.

Another Protestant church, which broke away from the Anglican Church in the 18th century under the Wesley brothers, is the Methodist Church. A term you may hear used about Methodists is that they are 'nonconformists', who worship independently from the established Church of England. Other 'non-conformist' churches include Baptist, Quaker, United Reformed, and Presbyterian churches.

In the late 19th century Pentecostalism emerged, moving away from more traditional forms of Christianity and worshipping in more spontaneous and lively ways with a focus on the Holy Spirit. Another more recent Christian denomination is the Salvation Army, which emerged in the late 1800s with an emphasis on practical responses to the needs of the homeless and most vulnerable.

Your local area might have independent evangelical or Brethren churches. Depending on your context, there may be Orthodox churches (such as Greek Orthodox or Russian Orthodox). There are also Black majority churches, such as the Redeemed Christian Church of God, with lively gospel music, and increasingly common are churches that don't own a building and which meet in local schools or community centres.

Even within these different groups there is wide variety. In the Church of England, for example, there are 'Anglo-Catholic' parishes and others that are described as 'low church', with less formality. Christian churches work together on the ground, sometimes through a group called Churches Together. They might hold joint events or work together on community projects. They (mostly) value and respect their differences.

How denominations differ

To explain why residents might wish to link with their own denomination, it is helpful to understand some of the differences between groups.

- **Formality** – some churches have set prayers and services (also called 'liturgies') which are said at different times. These prayers have been written down, and there may be specific prayers that are said each day. Other churches are more spontaneous and have less focus on the church calendar and seasons. Prayers are not written down but said spontaneously in the moment. In some churches special clothes are worn by those who are leading and perhaps also those who are singing, whereas in other churches everyone wears the same kind of clothes. In some churches people dress very smartly; in others the dress code is casual. When your residents were younger, it is likely people wore their 'Sunday best' for church, and even a hat. This is becoming less typical.

- **Leadership and titles** – some churches have a leadership hierarchy – priests, archdeacons, and bishops in the Roman Catholic and Anglican churches, for instance – whereas other churches have a group who run the church together, without necessarily a full-time paid person. You may be aware that in some churches, women cannot be in leadership positions. The names church leaders are given differ, too; priest, elder, pastor, deacon, and minister are all titles given to church leaders. Special training and careful selection are needed to be 'ordained' and be given the title Reverend.

- **Rituals** – some churches have elaborate rituals that form part of worship, which might involve lighting candles, burning incense, and ringing bells. For other churches, these rituals are seen as unnecessary in approaching God.

- **Traditions** – some churches hold to old, well-established patterns of Christian worship, with a robed choir and organ for hymn singing. Other churches mainly sing modern worship songs accompanied by a band.

Case study

Agatha

Agatha's Christian heritage was a rich mix of traditions. Growing up in St Lucia, she attended a Pentecostal church with her parents. When she came to the UK, she became established within a New Testament Church of God in Birmingham. Later in life she moved to be closer to her daughter and grandchildren in Wales, where she settled in a Baptist church. Her daughter's partner is Roman Catholic, and the children are being raised in the Catholic Church. Agatha is happy to worship with other Christians anywhere she senses the people around her share her love for God and commitment to social justice.

Throughout her life she has volunteered through church on projects reaching out to families on low incomes. For Agatha, being a Christian has to be reflected in how you treat those who are marginalised. She looks out for those in her care home who are new and seem isolated.

Non-orthodox groups and other faiths

The major Christian denominations all agree on key beliefs. As mentioned above, they all agree that the Creed is the true statement of the Christian faith.

There are other religious organisations which hold to some of the beliefs of Christianity but are not seen by other Christian denominations as 'orthodox'. They might not believe in the Trinity, where God is seen as 'three persons in one' (Father, Son, and Holy Spirit). They may not believe in the divinity of Jesus as the Son of God. These churches include The Unitarians, Spiritualists, Jehovah's Witnesses, Christian Science, and The Church of Jesus Christ of Latter-day Saints (also known as the Mormon Church). You may have residents who belong to these groups and wish to maintain their links with this community of faith.

A Christian religious leader would not be well placed to respond to the religious needs of residents of other faiths, but might help you connect with the person's community and enable visits from those who share their beliefs. There is mutual respect between the major world religions, and many commonly held values, such as peace and loving your neighbour.

It would not be wise to hold a combined act of worship, however, for orthodox and non-orthodox believers, or to assign as chaplain a non-orthodox person to an orthodox Christian, or vice versa. Similarly, residents would expect religious care to be provided by a representative of their own community, not a person who holds a different faith. Being person-centred includes arranging appropriate spiritual and religious care. A culture of mutual respect and acceptance can also be encouraged in a care home through marking important religious festivals through the year as an opportunity to learn about one another's religious and cultural heritage.

In conclusion

Churches and other faith communities can be a valuable source of enrichment not only for residents and staff who belong to them, but to the care home community as a whole. They not only enable care homes to provide religious and spiritual care, but also bring local connections and a sense of belonging within the wider community.

How to take care of yourself

The Revd Sally Rees

What is stress?

What makes a situation stressful is different for each of us. A certain degree of stimulation is needed every day to motivate us to lead fulfilling lives and to achieve our goals. A situation becomes stressful when there is more stimulation in a day (or over a longer time period) than we can cope with. So 'good' stress is a balance of optimum stimulation for each of us, and that will vary from person to person.

When we think of being stressed, we are usually referring to more stimulation than suits our individual needs, and too much stress can cause us to feel unwell.

This chapter is intended to be practical in nature and hopefully of real help to those fulfilling caring roles day after day which may generate stress, either through a difficult day or pressure accumulating over a period of caring duties. Stress can affect our bodies, minds, emotions, and spirits. As difficult as these things are sometimes to express, we will look at each of these separately.

Stress and the body

You will have heard that the normal physical response to stress is either 'fight or flight'. When we cannot run away from stress and it is not something we can fight, our bodies react in a number of physical ways.

The symptoms may include:

- In the cardiovascular system: tightness in the chest or a pounding heartbeat
- In the digestive system: nausea, sickness, and loss of appetite
- In the muscles: aching or tense muscles
- Headaches
- Disturbed sleep
- Inability to concentrate fully

First of all, it is good just to recognise these symptoms, as we can then act to address them with simple measures. For some people, it helps to do something that you know is positive, but some of us just need to stop for a while. So be kind to yourself. It may be that a mixture of easily doable measures – and relaxing or having an extra snooze – are all needed.

Take daily exercise

This keeps the heart healthy, loosens tense muscles, and lifts our mood. Choose exercise you enjoy. This can be as simple as taking a stroll outside, with or without a dog. It might be dancing or skipping – whatever you fancy!

Plan meals and eat as well as your circumstances allow

If possible, eat well-balanced meals at regular intervals and avoid having too much sugar, which can make your blood sugar unstable and cause additional stress to your body.

Use simple relaxation techniques

- A long soak in the bath (with or without bubbles) can help you to unwind and can ease sore or tense muscles.
- Relaxing before bed may help you settle to sleep. Try sipping a hot milky drink, or taking comfort from a hot water bottle or a soothing lavender bag.

- Read something that gives you pleasure.
- Use a simple relaxing exercise (an example is given in appendix VII, page 155).

Stress and mental well-being

Stress can affect our thoughts and feelings. Symptoms may include:

- Racing thoughts and an inability to 'switch off'
- Difficulty organising thoughts
- Lack of concentration and difficulty making decisions
- Lack of self-confidence
- Excessive worry and negative thinking
- A loss of perspective on issues, making 'a mountain out of a molehill', or driving yourself too hard
- Mood swings

Note: If you feel really unwell physically or mentally, do seek medical help. GPs see a lot of people who are stressed, and they can refer you to a counsellor, if necessary, or may advise medication, or both.

You are the one person who probably knows best what makes you feel stressed and how best to deal with it. Try to identify the cause of your stress and recognise changes to your normal thoughts and feelings.

Some helpful tips:

- Be kind to yourself. You are not superman or superwoman. Accept that these are difficult times.
- Give yourself a 'pat on the back' for getting through a hard day, for doing something difficult, or for doing something really well with limited time and resources.
- Try to accept how you truly feel, but also try to recognise when you need help. Asking for help is *not* a failing.
- Share your thoughts with a friend, partner, or pet. Stroke your cat or cuddle your dog.

- You may find mindfulness exercises helpful. They are an easy, accessible way to help thoughts settle and to calm the mind. (A mindfulness exercise can be found in appendix VII, page 158.)
- Try praying to God for his peace.

Stress and emotions

Stressed thoughts and feelings can lead to emotional stress. We might feel irritable, angry, depressed, anxious, hyperactive, or underactive. We may experience an increase in feelings of guilt, and we may have wild mood swings. In times of stress, it is normal to feel these things – they are all normal emotional responses. However, these feelings can lead to a change in behaviour. We may withdraw from others or we may feel impatient. We may feel angry and have the urge to express that anger.

We might also turn to some unhealthy ways of trying to manage our difficult feelings. These behaviours can include excessive alcohol intake, taking recreational drugs, and self-harming.

How we deal with emotions is as different as we are as individuals. Some might want to withdraw and be quiet or reflective. Some might find a degree of calm by immersing themselves in a book, listening to music, or watching a film.

Others might need to let their emotions out, to release some of the frustration. There are many healthy ways to do so.

Some helpful tips:

- Talk to someone and share your feelings and thoughts
- Write your feelings down. Acknowledge them and then throw the paper away
- Try writing a poem or doing some painting, drawing, or colouring
- Listen to music (you might find that loud, energetic music helps you to unwind or you may prefer relaxing, calming sounds)

- Shout out loud if you need to. Punch a pillow or squeeze a stress ball
- Try shouting at God – the psalmists did a lot of that. Many people believe that God hears our shouting and comes alongside us to help us in our time of need

Stress and the spirit

The spirit is a wide-ranging concept, but it can chiefly be thought of as the non-physical part of a person, which is the seat of emotions and character. The soul similarly is the sum of the invisible characteristics that make you *you*. It's the part of us that cries out the 'Why?' questions and seeks to make meaning out of difficulties. It's the part of us that is immortal, however we may define this. Living through stressful situations can cause us to become spiritually deflated.

You may not believe in God or that we are 'made in his image', but most of us are in tune with our spiritual side and feel connected to something outside ourselves, whether we call it 'a higher being', nature, or the universe. This connection to God, or whatever we might call it, helps us to understand different kinds of longings, such as the need to be creative, the need for love, the need to belong, and the need to care and be cared for.

Some of us also need to connect privately, or with others, in worship. We can also feel fulfilled by using our own creative gifts. It's another way to express ourselves and connect with God.

Often our 'love needs' are met when we are caring for others. We may find real fulfilment in doing a good job, seeing a resident respond with a smile, and so on. It is also good to remember that in the midst of stressful circumstances, we can look outside ourselves to a loving God and/or connect with creation.

Some suggestions to refresh your spirit:

- Connect, talk to, and share with those whom you love and who love you as best as you can in whatever circumstances.
- Experience something creative – walk and wonder at the creation, for example, and study a tree, flower, or bird.
- Cuddle a pet.
- Create something for yourself or someone else by sewing or knitting or a similar craft (bake a cake or take a photo).
- Read a novel or write some creative prose yourself.
- Listen to music or play an instrument.
- Sing something you love (it doesn't have to be in tune!).
- Find joy in something unexpected and have a good laugh!
- Read or listen to verses/passages of the Bible.
- Pray, silently or aloud, then quietly listen to God whispering to you.
- Rest and just 'be'.

Case study

Gemma

Gemma first started working in Tall Trees as a volunteer when she was in sixth form. She loved the residents and applied for a paid post when she left school. Alongside studying for qualifications in care, she worked as a carer at Tall Trees.

The first few weeks were particularly busy at the home and, although she loved it, it was a time of huge learning, and she was really tired between shifts. Residents loved Gemma and joked that it was like having another granddaughter! They were very nurturing and encouraging of her as she gradually found her feet and grew in confidence. The warmth in Gemma's bonds with residents was what got her up in the morning for her shifts.

When longstanding resident Nellie died a few weeks after Gemma started in role, she was devastated. It was the first death of someone close that Gemma had gone through, and it knocked her for six.

Her team leader Sheila recognised the impact of this bereavement on her promising new carer; she spent time with Gemma when she came on shift and first heard the news, helping her work through the grief over losing Nellie. She reassured her it was normal to feel deeply when a resident you have cared for dies and that she would find ways to cope with the deaths that would happen in the future.

Sheila rang the manager to ask if Gemma could go home at lunch-time when most of the heavy duties were done. Gemma already had the following two days scheduled as time off. At lunch-time Gemma went home early as agreed. She cried with her mum as she shared the news Nellie had died, then had a sandwich and went to bed, sleeping through to the next morning.

On her days off Gemma met up with her best friend for a walk in the park and shared lovely memories of Nellie over a coffee in their favourite café. This helped Gemma see how much Nellie had helped her as well as how close they were, meaning she could feel thankful alongside the sadness. She built in extra 'down time' during the days off, watching her favourite film which sparked some more tears.

After Gemma's days off, she was able to face work again and felt she had enough resilience to give her energy and attention to her other residents. She also spent time talking with colleagues about Nellie.

Be kind

Finally, remember to be kind to yourself. Give yourself at least one little treat each day (perhaps a chocolate, a soak in the bath, or a book).

If it would be helpful for you, make a five-point plan to try to help you keep your body, mind, and spirit positive each day, and help you cope with stress. Try to include something for each of the parts that make you *you*, both in your eyes and in God's eyes. Here is an example of a five-point plan:

1 Talk to one person who is important to you and share about your day
2 Think of one positive or joyful thing (it may be a memory) that you love and hold that thought in your mind whenever you can throughout your day
3 If you feel up to it, take one form of exercise that you can manage
4 Experience one creative thing – wonder at something beautiful; take a photo; sing a song; spend some time in worship
5 Take time to 'be' and get some rest

If you would like more support, please feel free to contact your Anna Chaplain, minister, or pastoral visitor.

In conclusion

In a role where you are constantly responding to the needs of other human beings who depend on you, it is easy to lose sight of your own needs. Rates of staff turnover in the care home sector are high, with 30% of care sector employees leaving their jobs every year. There are many factors contributing to this high turnover, but one is burnout, often exacerbated by difficulties recruiting to vacancies and team members having to work extra shifts.

In this context, attending to the physical, emotional, mental, and spiritual impact of care work on those delivering services to our growing frail elderly population is essential. Making space for self-care is vital for the flourishing of all those who see care as their vocation, and whose commitment makes a profound difference to the lives of older people. But it is also critical if we are to sustain a dynamic care sector into the future.

Closing remarks

Julia Burton-Jones

Whether you have dipped into this book as needed or have been reading every chapter, we hope it has enabled you to reflect on aspects of life which can be lost in our busy world as we focus on what needs to be done each day rather than the promptings of our inner lives.

The first chapter looked at what is meant by spiritual and religious care and the requirements placed on care homes to enable spirituality and faith to be expressed. How might we assess and record spiritual and religious needs in the process of care planning and delivery?

In the second and third chapters, the focus was on facilitating worship – with individual and groups of residents. Christian worship may provide strength, comfort, and structure for residents. How might care homes offer dedicated spaces for residents to pray individually or gather for church services? What are typical components of Christian worship, such as singing, reading the Bible, and praying? Chapter 5 described the beliefs and rituals that are important to Christian residents and explained why regular opportunities for practices like taking Holy Communion have been an essential element of the rhythm of life for some residents who will naturally wish them to continue after moving into a care home.

The focus of chapter 5 was the conversations and behaviours that can support a resident who is dying; music, readings, and prayers that might be a spiritual comfort were listed. In chapter 6 we outlined ways to enable residents and staff to say goodbye to a person they have loved when unable to attend their funeral – a sensitive, personalised memorial service can offer a much-needed ritual of remembrance which supports those who are grieving.

Chapter 7 suggested creative approaches to spiritual care, whatever a person believes. Ways to enable individuals to express their innermost thoughts and feelings and connect with others and the world around them are many and varied. In the eighth chapter, ideas for connecting positively with local churches and faith groups were outlined to help in bringing spiritual care and community engagement into the care home.

Finally, chapter 9 drew attention to the spiritual needs of the care-givers – the staff who work in care homes. In a working environment that can be stressful and where you are constantly giving out, self-care and noticing signs of burnout in your body are vital.

In considering the spiritual longings of your residents, perhaps you will take time to nurture your own soul and give space to those things which lift your spirit and make your heart sing, be that sitting in the garden feeling the sun on your face, dancing to your favourite music, or attending your own place of worship if you are a person of faith.

Identifying and responding to residents' spiritual and religious needs will then not feel like an extra task to be completed or a pressure on top of what can already feel like demanding work, but a role which brings meaning and sparks satisfaction in your work caring for older people. Discovering what is most important to residents is a quest which brings you closer to them and can help you recognise your shared humanity and the wisdom older people bring to our communities.

A key message of this book is that you don't need to be someone who sees themselves as deeply spiritual or religious to help meet residents' spiritual and religious needs. We can all play our part. Reading religious readings, prayers, or poems that bring comfort to a resident who is woken by a bad dream and feels vulnerable in the middle of the night is a simple way to meet profound needs. Enabling a resident to listen to the music which connects them with their earlier life honours their individuality and is part of good spiritual care.

You don't need to be on the care team to get involved; each member of staff makes connections with residents and can spend time with them sharing their life and discovering common interests and values.

We hope you will feel comfortable in facilitating Christian conversations and services with the resources included here, but also that you will be confident in reaching out to local churches and other religious communities to work with you to bring friendship, community connections, and religious care into your care home. As we grow the Anna Chaplaincy network across the UK, we hope an increasing number of care homes will have someone to call upon who is dedicated to the spiritual care of older people living there.

If you are in a management role in the care sector, we invite you to consider who in your team might be a spiritual care lead, holding responsibility in this area of holistic care and linking with faith and community organisations that can help. If you have staff members who belong to different faith groups, they are your key to understanding residents who also belong to those groups. They can help the staff team show sensitivity and may be trusted by residents to give support in practising their faith, enabling them to keep in touch with their religious community.

As a movement, Anna Chaplaincy recognises the commitment of all those who work in this vital sector. Every day we see staff members going above and beyond to cherish some of our frailest and most vulnerable citizens. The danger of exhaustion is all too real, and we acknowledge the cost that can come with choosing this career path, but without a strong and resilient workforce the risk to our ageing population is vast. Where Anna Chaplains develop relationships with care homes, they seek to be chaplains to the staff who work there, as well as residents and visitors. And they can tell the stories of heroic kindness and loving tenderness shown by care staff that go largely unseen. They can champion the role your teams fulfil. So, we look forward to continuing to build a positive and fruitful relationship with you in the years to come, as we learn together how best to provide whole-person care.

Appendix I: Familiar hymns

All things bright and beautiful

All things bright and beautiful,
all creatures great and small,
all things wise and wonderful,
the Lord God made them all.

Each little flow'r that opens,
each little bird that sings,
he made their glowing colours,
he made their tiny wings.

All things bright and beautiful…

The purple-headed mountain,
the river running by,
the sunset, and the morning,
that brightens up the sky.

All things bright and beautiful…

The cold wind in the winter,
the pleasant summer sun,
the ripe fruits in the garden:
he made them, every one.

All things bright and beautiful…

He gave us eyes to see them,
and lips that we might tell
how great is God Almighty,
who has made all things well.

All things bright and beautiful...

Amazing grace

Amazing grace, how sweet the sound
that saved a wretch like me!
I once was lost, but now am found,
was blind, but now I see.

'Twas grace that taught my heart to fear,
and grace my fears relieved;
how precious did that grace appear
the hour I first believed!

Through many dangers, toils and snares
I have already come:
'tis grace has brought me safe thus far,
and grace will lead me home.

The Lord has promised good to me,
his word my hope secures;
he will my shield and portion be
as long as life endures.

Yes, when this flesh and heart shall fail,
and mortal life shall cease:
I shall possess, within the veil,
a life of joy and peace.

The earth shall soon dissolve like snow,
the sun forbear to shine;

but God, who called me here below,
will be forever mine.

He's got the whole world in his hands

He's got the whole world in his hands,
He's got the whole world in his hands,
He's got the whole world in his hands,
He's got the whole world in his hands!

He's got you and me sister/brother in his hands (x3)
He's got the whole world in his hands!

He's got the little tiny baby in his hands (x3)
He's got the whole world in his hands!

He's got everybody here in his hands (x3)
He's got the whole world in his hands!

Be thou my vision

Be thou my vision, O Lord of my heart;
naught be all else to me save that thou art;
thou my best thought by day or by night;
waking or sleeping, thy presence my light.

Be thou my wisdom, be thou my true word;
I ever with thee and thou with me, Lord;
thou my great Father, and I thy true son;
thou in me dwelling, and I with thee one.

Be thou my breastplate, my sword for the fight;
be thou my dignity, thou my delight.
Thou my soul's shelter, thou my high tower;
raise thou me heavenward, O power of my power.

Riches I heed not, nor vain, empty praise;
thou mine inheritance, now and always.
Thou and thou only, first in my heart,
High King of Heaven, my treasure thou art.

High King of Heaven, my victory won,
may I reach Heaven's joys, O bright Heav'ns Sun!
Heart of my heart, whatever befall,
still be my vision, O ruler of all.

Jesus loves me, this I know

Jesus loves me, this I know,
for the Bible tells me so.
Little ones to him belong;
they are weak but he is strong.

Yes, Jesus loves me!
Yes, Jesus loves me!
Yes, Jesus loves me!
The Bible tells me so.

Jesus bids us shine with a pure, clear light

Jesus bids us shine with a pure, clear light,
like a little candle burning in the night.
In this world of darkness, so let us shine –
you in your small corner, and I in mine.

Jesus bids us shine, first of all for him;
well he sees and knows it, if our light is dim;
he looks down from heaven, sees us shine –
you in your small corner, and I in mine.

Jesus bids us shine, then; for all around
many kinds of darkness in this world abound:
sin and want and sorrow: we must shine –
you in your small corner, and I in mine.

What a friend we have in Jesus

What a friend we have in Jesus,
all our sins and griefs to bear!
What a privilege to carry
everything to God in prayer!
O what peace we often forfeit,
O what needless pain we bear,
all because we do not carry
everything to God in prayer!

Have we trials and temptations?
Is there trouble anywhere?
We should never be discouraged;
take it to the Lord in prayer!
Can we find a friend so faithful
who will all our sorrows share?
Jesus knows our every weakness;
take it to the Lord in prayer!

Are we weak and heavy laden,
cumbered with a load of care?
Precious Saviour, still our refuge –
take it to the Lord in prayer!
Do your friends despise, forsake you?
Take it to the Lord in prayer!
In his arms he'll take and shield you;
you will find a solace there.

Guide me, O thou great Redeemer

Guide me, O thou great Redeemer,
pilgrim through this barren land;
I am weak but thou art mighty;
hold me with thy powerful hand:
Bread of heaven, bread of heaven,
feed me till I want no more.

Open now the crystal fountain,
whence the healing streams doth flow;
let the fiery, cloudy pillar,
lead me all my journey through:
Strong deliverer, strong deliverer
Be thou still my strength and shield.

When I tread the verge of Jordan,
bid my anxious fears subside;
death of death, and hell's destruction,
land me safe on Canaan's side;
songs of praises, songs of praises,
I will ever give to thee.

Resources that can be purchased

- Hymn book and CD: *Hymns We've Always Loved* (published by Kevin Mayhew), available both as a CD and a large-print hymn book
- CD: *50 Hymns in Lower Keys* (also published by Kevin Mayhew)
- Various CDs of hymns sung by choirs and other popular artists.

Appendix II: Bible readings

These can be used in individual or group worship.

Psalm 23 – The shepherd psalm

The Lord is my shepherd, I lack nothing.
  He makes me lie down in green pastures,
he leads me beside quiet waters,
  he refreshes my soul.
He guides me along the right paths
  for his name's sake.
Even though I walk
  through the darkest valley,
I will fear no evil,
  for you are with me;
your rod and your staff,
  they comfort me.

You prepare a table before me
  in the presence of my enemies.
You anoint my head with oil;
  my cup overflows.
Surely your goodness and love will follow me
  all the days of my life,
and I will dwell in the house of the Lord
  forever.

Psalm 27 – A song of confidence in God's protection

The Lord is my light and my salvation –
  whom shall I fear?
The Lord is the stronghold of my life –
  of whom shall I be afraid?

When the wicked advance against me
  to devour me,
it is my enemies and my foes
  who will stumble and fall.
Though an army besiege me,
  my heart will not fear;
though war break out against me,
  even then I will be confident.

One thing I ask from the Lord,
  this only do I seek:
that I may dwell in the house of the Lord
  all the days of my life,
to gaze on the beauty of the Lord
  and to seek him in his temple.
For in the day of trouble
  he will keep me safe in his dwelling;
he will hide me in the shelter of his sacred tent
  and set me high upon a rock.

Then my head will be exalted
  above the enemies who surround me;
at his sacred tent I will sacrifice with shouts of joy;
  I will sing and make music to the Lord.

Hear my voice when I call, Lord;
  be merciful to me and answer me.
My heart says of you, 'Seek his face!'
  Your face, Lord, I will seek.
Do not hide your face from me,

do not turn your servant away in anger;
you have been my helper.
Do not reject me or forsake me,
God my Saviour.
Though my father and mother forsake me,
the Lord will receive me.
Teach me your way, Lord;
lead me in a straight path
because of my oppressors.
Do not hand me over to the desire of my foes,
for false witnesses rise up against me,
spouting malicious accusations.

I remain confident of this:
I will see the goodness of the Lord
in the land of the living.
Wait for the Lord;
be strong and take heart
and wait for the Lord.

Psalm 121 – Looking to God for help

I lift up my eyes to the mountains –
where does my help come from?
My help comes from the Lord,
the Maker of heaven and earth.

He will not let your foot slip –
he who watches over you will not slumber;
indeed, he who watches over Israel
will neither slumber nor sleep.

The Lord watches over you –
the Lord is your shade at your right hand;
the sun will not harm you by day,
nor the moon by night.

The Lord will keep you from all harm –
 he will watch over your life;
the Lord will watch over your coming and going
 both now and forevermore.

Psalm 139 – God made us and knows us

You have searched me, Lord,
 and you know me.
You know when I sit and when I rise;
 you perceive my thoughts from afar.
You discern my going out and my lying down;
 you are familiar with all my ways.
Before a word is on my tongue
 you, Lord, know it completely.
You hem me in behind and before,
 and you lay your hand upon me.
Such knowledge is too wonderful for me,
 too lofty for me to attain.

Where can I go from your Spirit?
 Where can I flee from your presence?
If I go up to the heavens, you are there;
 if I make my bed in the depths, you are there.
If I rise on the wings of the dawn,
 if I settle on the far side of the sea,
even there your hand will guide me,
 your right hand will hold me fast.
If I say, 'Surely the darkness will hide me
 and the light become night around me,'
even the darkness will not be dark to you;
 the night will shine like the day,
 for darkness is as light to you.

For you created my inmost being;
  you knit me together in my mother's womb.
I praise you because I am fearfully and wonderfully made;
  your works are wonderful,
  I know that full well.
My frame was not hidden from you
  when I was made in the secret place,
  when I was woven together in the depths of the earth.
Your eyes saw my unformed body;
  all the days ordained for me were written in your book
  before one of them came to be.
How precious to me are your thoughts, God!
  How vast is the sum of them!
Were I to count them,
  they would outnumber the grains of sand –
  when I awake, I am still with you.

If only you, God, would slay the wicked!
  Away from me, you who are bloodthirsty!
They speak of you with evil intent;
  your adversaries misuse your name.
Do I not hate those who hate you, Lord,
  and abhor those who are in rebellion against you?
I have nothing but hatred for them;
  I count them my enemies.
Search me, God, and know my heart;
  test me and know my anxious thoughts.
See if there is any offensive way in me,
  and lead me in the way everlasting.

1 Corinthians 13 – The gift of love

If I speak in the tongues of men or of angels, but do not have love, I am only a resounding gong or a clanging cymbal. If I have the gift of prophecy and can fathom all mysteries and all knowledge, and if I have a faith that can move mountains, but do not have love, I am nothing. If I give all I possess to the poor and give over my body to hardship that I may boast, but do not have love, I gain nothing.

Love is patient, love is kind. It does not envy, it does not boast, it is not proud. It does not dishonour others, it is not self-seeking, it is not easily angered, it keeps no record of wrongs. Love does not delight in evil but rejoices with the truth. It always protects, always trusts, always hopes, always perseveres.

Love never fails. But where there are prophecies, they will cease; where there are tongues, they will be stilled; where there is knowledge, it will pass away. For we know in part and we prophesy in part, but when completeness comes, what is in part disappears. When I was a child, I talked like a child, I thought like a child, I reasoned like a child. When I became a man, I put the ways of childhood behind me. For now we see only a reflection as in a mirror; then we shall see face to face. Now I know in part; then I shall know fully, even as I am fully known.

And now these three remain: faith, hope and love. But the greatest of these is love.

John 14:1–7 – Jesus, the way to the Father

'Do not let your hearts be troubled. You believe in God; believe also in me. My Father's house has many rooms; if that were not so, would I have told you that I am going there to prepare a place for you? And if I go and prepare a place for you, I will come back and take you to be with me that you also may be where I am. You know the way to the place where I am going.'

Thomas said to him, 'Lord, we don't know where you are going, so how can we know the way?'

Jesus answered, 'I am the way and the truth and the life. No one comes to the Father except through me. If you really know me, you will know my Father as well. From now on, you do know him and have seen him.'

Revelation 21:1–5 – A new heaven and a new earth

Then I saw 'a new heaven and a new earth', for the first heaven and the first earth had passed away, and there was no longer any sea. I saw the Holy City, the new Jerusalem, coming down out of heaven from God, prepared as a bride beautifully dressed for her husband. And I heard a loud voice from the throne saying, 'Look! God's dwelling-place is now among the people, and he will dwell with them. They will be his people, and God himself will be with them and be their God. "He will wipe every tear from their eyes. There will be no more death" or mourning or crying or pain, for the old order of things has passed away.'

He who was seated on the throne said, 'I am making everything new!' Then he said, 'Write this down, for these words are trustworthy and true.'

Ecclesiastes 3:1–14 – Everything has its time

There is a time for everything,
and a season for every activity under the heavens:
a time to be born and a time to die,
a time to plant and a time to uproot,
a time to kill and a time to heal,
a time to tear down and a time to build,
a time to weep and a time to laugh,
a time to mourn and a time to dance,
a time to scatter stones and a time to gather them,
a time to embrace and a time to refrain from embracing,
a time to search and a time to give up,
a time to keep and a time to throw away,
a time to tear and a time to mend,
a time to be silent and a time to speak,
a time to love and a time to hate,
a time for war and a time for peace.

What do workers gain from their toil? I have seen the burden God has laid on the human race. He has made everything beautiful in its time. He has also set eternity in the human heart; yet no one can fathom what God has done from beginning to end. I know that there is nothing better for people than to be happy and to do good while they live. That each of them may eat and drink, and find satisfaction in all their toil – this is the gift of God. I know that everything God does will endure forever; nothing can be added to it and nothing taken from it. God does it so that people will fear him.

Luke 19:1–10 – Zacchaeus, the story of a short man who wanted to see Jesus

Jesus entered Jericho and was passing through. A man was there by the name of Zacchaeus; he was a chief tax collector and was wealthy. He wanted to see who Jesus was, but because he was short he could not see over the crowd. So he ran ahead and climbed a sycamore-fig tree to see him, since Jesus was coming that way.

When Jesus reached the spot, he looked up and said to him, 'Zacchaeus, come down immediately. I must stay at your house today.' So he came down at once and welcomed him gladly.

All the people saw this and began to mutter, 'He has gone to be the guest of a sinner.'

But Zacchaeus stood up and said to the Lord, 'Look, Lord! Here and now I give half of my possessions to the poor, and if I have cheated anybody out of anything, I will pay back four times the amount.'

Jesus said to him, 'Today salvation has come to this house, because this man, too, is a son of Abraham. For the Son of Man came to seek and to save the lost.'

Matthew 4:18–22 – Jesus calls his first disciples

As Jesus was walking beside the Sea of Galilee, he saw two brothers, Simon called Peter and his brother Andrew. They were casting a net into the lake, for they were fishermen. 'Come, follow me,' Jesus said, 'and I will send you out to fish for people.' At once they left their nets and followed him.

Going on from there, he saw two other brothers, James son of Zebedee and his brother John. They were in a boat with their father Zebedee, preparing their nets. Jesus called them, and immediately they left the boat and their father and followed him.

Bible reading notes and reflections

Bible Reflections for Older People is published every four months by BRF Ministries. Each issue contains 40 Bible reflections and prayer suggestions, written by older people for older people, to use and revisit as often as needed. Find out more at **brfresources.org.uk/collections/bible-reflections-for-older-people**.

BRF Ministries also has other Bible reading notes; see **brfresources.org.uk/our-notes**.

Eddie Askew's books of prayers and meditations, published by Leprosy Mission International, resonate with older people and are available through second-hand booksellers:

- *A Silence and a Shouting* (1982)
- *Disguises of Love* (1983)
- *Facing the Storm* (1989)
- *Cross Purposes* (1995)
- *Music on the Wind* (1998)
- *Unexpected Journeys* (2002)
- *Encounters* (2004)

Appendix III: Prayers

The Serenity Prayer

God, grant me the serenity to accept the things I cannot change, courage to change the things I can, and wisdom to know the difference.

The Grace

May the grace of our Lord Jesus Christ, and the love of God, and the fellowship of the Holy Spirit, be with us all evermore. Amen.

The Aaronic blessing

May the Lord bless you and keep you;
May the Lord make his face shine on you and be gracious to you;
May the Lord turn his face towards you and give you peace.

The Lord's Prayer

Our Father, who art in heaven,
hallowed be thy name;
thy kingdom come;
thy will be done;
on earth as it is in heaven.
Give us this day our daily bread.

And forgive us our trespasses,
as we forgive those who trespass against us.
And lead us not into temptation;
but deliver us from evil.
For thine is the kingdom,
the power, and the glory,
forever and ever. Amen.

Compline prayer – Lighten our darkness

Lighten our darkness, Lord, we pray,
and in your great mercy
defend us from all perils and dangers of this night,
for the love of your only Son, our Saviour Jesus Christ.

The Jesus Prayer

Lord Jesus Christ,
Son of God,
have mercy on me,
a sinner.

Prayer of St Francis of Assisi

Lord, make me an instrument of your peace:
where there is hatred, let me sow love;
where there is injury, pardon;
where there is doubt, faith;
where there is despair, hope;
where there is darkness, light;

where there is sadness, joy.
O Divine Master, grant that I may not so much seek
to be consoled, as to console,
to be understood, as to understand,
to be loved, as to love.
For it is in giving that we receive,
it is in pardoning that we are pardoned,
and it is in dying that we are born to eternal life.

A prayer from St Patrick

Christ with me,
Christ before me,
Christ behind me,
Christ in me,
Christ beneath me,
Christ above me,
Christ on my right,
Christ on my left,
Christ when I lie down,
Christ when I arise,
Christ in the heart of every person who thinks of me,
Christ in every eye that sees me,
Christ in the ear that hears me.

Prayer of Charles de Foucauld

Father, I abandon myself into your hands.
Do with me what you will.
Whatever you may do, I thank you:
I am ready for all, I accept all.
Let only your will be done in me,
and in all your creatures –
I wish no more than this, O Lord.
Into your hands I commend my soul;

I offer it to you with all the love of my heart,
for I love you, Lord, and so need to give myself,
to surrender myself into your hands without reserve,
and with boundless confidence,
for you are my Father.

Prayer of St Richard of Chichester

Thanks be to you, our Lord Jesus Christ,
for all the benefits you have given us,
for all the pains and insults you have borne for us.
Most merciful Redeemer, Friend, and Brother,
may we know you more clearly,
love you more dearly,
and follow you more nearly,
day by day. Amen.

A prayer from St Anselm

O Lord our God,
grant us grace to desire you with our whole heart,
that so desiring, we may seek and find you;
and so finding you we may love you;
and loving you we may hate those sins
from which you have redeemed us,
for the sake of Jesus Christ.

A prayer from St Ignatius of Loyola

Fill us, we pray, with your light and life
that we may show forth your wondrous glory.
Grant that your love may so fill our hearts

that we may count nothing too small to do for you,
nothing too much to give,
and nothing too hard to bear.

A prayer from St Columba

O Lord,
in the name of Jesus Christ your Son our Lord
give us that love which can never cease,
that will kindle our lamps but not extinguish them,
that they may burn in us and enlighten others.
O Christ, our dearest Saviour,
kindle our lamps,
that they may evermore shine in your temple,
that they may receive unquenchable light from you
that will enlighten our darkness,
and lessen the darkness of the world.

A prayer from St Augustine

O Lord our God,
fill us with hope in the shadow of your wings,
protect and sustain us.
You will uphold us, right from our childhood to our old age,
because our present strength,
if it comes from you, is strength indeed;
but if it is merely our own strength then it is weakness.
When we are close to you we find living goodness,
but at the very moment we turn aside from you
we become corrupt.
So, Lord, make us retrace our steps,
so that we are not defeated.

Collect from Common Worship (Thursday morning)

O God, the author of peace and lover of concord,
to know you is eternal life,
to serve you is perfect freedom:
defend us your servants from all assaults of our enemies,
that we may trust in your defence
and not fear the power of any adversaries;
through Jesus Christ our Lord. Amen.

A Gaelic blessing

May the road rise up to meet you,
may the wind be always at your back,
may the sunshine warm upon your face,
the rains fall soft upon your fields,
and until we meet again,
may God hold you in the palm of his hand.

Methodist covenant prayer

I am no longer my own but yours.
Your will, not mine, be done in all things,
wherever you may place me,
in all that I do
   and in all that I may endure;
when there is work for me
   and when there is none;
when I am troubled
   and when I am at peace.
Your will be done
when I am valued
   and when I am disregarded;

when I find fulfilment
and when it is lacking;
when I have all things,
and when I have nothing.
I willingly offer
all I have and am
to serve you,
as and where you choose.

Glorious and blessed God,
Father, Son, and Holy Spirit,
you are mine and I am yours.
May it be so forever.
Let this covenant now made on earth
be fulfilled in heaven. Amen.

Prevent us, O Lord

Prevent us, O Lord, in all our doings with thy most gracious favour, and further us with thy continual help; that in all our works, begun, continued, and ended in thee, we may glorify thy holy name, and finally by thy mercy obtain everlasting life; through Jesus Christ Our Lord. Amen.

African canticle

All you big things, bless the Lord.
Mount Kilimanjaro and Lake Victoria,
the Rift Valley and the Serengeti Plain,
fat boababs and shady mango trees,
bless the Lord.
Praise and extol him forever and ever.
All you tiny things, bless the Lord.

Busy black ants and hopping fleas,
wriggling tadpoles and mosquito larvae,
flying locusts and water drops,
pollen dust and tsetse flies,
millet seeds and dried dagga,
bless the Lord.
Praise and extol him forever and ever.

A psalm for Africa

O praise God in his holy place,
praise him in the sky our tent,
praise him in the earth our mother;
praise him for his mighty works,
praise him for his mighty power.
Praise him with the beating of great drums,
praise him with the horn and rattle;
praise him in the rhythm of the dance,
praise him in the clapping of the hands;
praise him in the stamping of the feet,
praise him in the singing of the chant.
Praise him with the rushing of great rivers,
praise him with the music of the wind;
praise him with the swaying of tall trees,
praise him with the singing of the sea.
Praise him, the one on whom we lean and do not fall;
let everything that has breath praise the Lord.

Celtic prayers

David Adam's *Landscapes of Light: An illustrated anthology of prayers* (SPCK, 2001) has numerous short prayers that may be suitable to use in a care home setting.

Messy Vintage activity

This activity is from a downloadable resource on the BRF Messy Vintage webpage.

You will need: 14 cm square boards cut from MDF board or other strong material; mosaic stone tiles; clear or aqua glass vase pebbles; strong adhesive.

Stick the tiles on to the boards, to represent your faith journey or a particular time during your life journey. Somewhere on the board, place one glass pebble, to represent a shining moment on your journey.

For more sessions and suggestions of activities for worship, visit **messychurch.org.uk/messy-vintage**.

Appendix IV: Sources of spiritual care and support

Daily Hope phone line

Daily Hope (0800 804 8044) is an excellent resource for anyone who wishes to worship but has no access to the internet. It is a free phone line offering hymns, reflections, and prayers. This number can be called at any time of the day or night and as often as required. If the individual in your care cannot use the phone, please dial the number for them. There are several options to choose from, depending on whether a hymn, reflection, prayer, or service is desired. The selections offered range from 5 to 20 minutes, depending on which option is chosen.

Websites with Christian prayers and reflections

- **sacredspace.com** – from the Jesuits of Ireland based on Ignatian spirituality (in many languages)
- **ignatianspirituality.com** – prayer from the Ignatian Christian tradition
- **faithandworship.com** – daily prayers, website created by Church of England lay minister John Birch

Embracing Age

Embracing Age (**embracingage.org.uk**) is a Christian organisation which links volunteer befrienders from churches with care homes for older people. It provides them with training and ensures they are DBS checked. It currently operates in the London borough of Richmond, the Isle of Wight, West Sussex, and Hampshire. It also has poetry books and a series of Bible reflections called *Making Moments*.

BRF Ministries

The home of Anna Chaplaincy, BRF Ministries is also a publisher of Christian books (such as this one!) and has many resources for prayer and meditation, including Bible reading notes such as *Bible Reflections for Older People* (published three times a year). These resources are available at **brfresources.org.uk**.

Spiritual Eldercare

Created by Elisa Bosley, a chaplain in the USA, **spiritualeldercare.com** has a wealth of free downloadable hymn tracks and sheets, worship resources, Bible studies, devotions, prayers, and other useful material.

The Iona Community

Wild Goose Publications (**ionabooks.com**) is where you find the music and prayer resources of the Iona Community, which are published in the Celtic tradition of St Columba. Many are available as digital downloads for a modest charge.

Lindisfarne

Lindisfarne is like Iona in being a place of Christian pilgrimage within the Celtic tradition. The Scriptorium (**lindisfarne-scriptorium.co.uk**) has downloadable colouring sheets, books of prayers, and prayer cards.

Kevin Mayhew

Kevin Mayhew (**kevinmayhew.com**) publishes *The Large Print Prayer Book: Favourite prayers, poems and Bible readings*. They also publish large print editions of *Hymns We've Always Loved* (to accompany the CD set) and *Catholic Hymns Old and New*.

Life Words

Free downloadable resources with Bible verses (**lifewords.global**).

Resources aimed at those living with dementia

- Weny Gleadle and Frances Attwood, *Dementia, God, and the Church: Journeying with hope* (BRF Ministries, 2026)
- Richard Behers, *Spiritual Care for People Living with Dementia Using Multisensory Interventions: A practical guide for chaplains* (Jessica Kingsley, 2018)
- Chris Coe, *Prayers for Those with Dementia* (Kevin Mayhew, 2011)
- Patrick Coghlan, *Creating Church at Home for Older People Living with Dementia* (Kevin Mayhew, 2016)

- Louise Morse (ed.), *Worshipping with Dementia: Meditations, scriptures and prayers for sufferers and carers* (Monarch Books, 2010)

- Siobhán O'Keeffe, *Petals of Prayer: Prayers, reflections and resources for people with dementia, and their carers* (Kevin Mayhew, 2011) – available as a book and DVD

- Lindsay Pelloquin and Jaye Keightley, *Celebrating the Seasons in Residential Care Homes: A service for every week of the year* (The Paul Thomas Group, 2022)

- Fay Sampson, *Prayers for Dementia: And how to live well with it* (Darton, Longman and Todd, 2017)

Appendix V: Sample services for a group of residents

Sample service 1 – God's love for us

For this service, you will need:

- *A single fresh flower with lots of petals*
- *Music for the two songs (although they could be sung without music)*
- *A large heart shape, cut from a piece of A4 red card*

Setting the scene

If possible, set up a table and cloth with some flowers, a battery-powered candle, a Bible, and a cross, if you have one.

Opening words

As we begin our short worship service, I will switch on the candle. This reminds us that the Lord is here and his Spirit is with us.

Song

'He's got the whole world in his hands' *(see appendix I, page 111).*

You don't need to provide written words for this song. Choose whatever verses you fancy – 'tiny little baby', 'everybody here' and so on, or make up your own verses, adding the names of residents. You could encourage the residents to do actions with you – make a circle with your arms then bring them round to cup your hands; rock the baby; point round the circle; and so on.

Today, the theme of our service is love *(hold up your red heart shape).* We'll start with a mini-quiz – can you finish the names of these famous couples?

- Romeo and… ? *(Juliet)*
- In the garden of Eden, there was Adam and… ? *(Eve)*
- Bonnie and… ? *(Clyde)*
- Antony and Cl… ? *(Cleopatra)*
- And a royal couple – William and… ? *(Kate)*

Who can finish this rhyme off – 'Roses are red, violets are blue, sugar is sweet, and so are… '? *(You)*

The Beatles sang, 'All you need is… '? *(Love)*

So it's love we're thinking about today, but especially God's love for each of us. We'll have a reading from the Bible now.

Bible reading

> You, Lord, are a compassionate and gracious God, slow to anger, abounding in love and faithfulness.
> PSALM 86:15

(Read twice.)

Reflection

We're thinking about love. What food do you love? *(Encourage answers.)* Who do (or did) you love? *(Allow time for some of the residents to tell you.)*

(Hold up a large daisy-type flower.) I wonder if you ever used to do this… *(Start to pull a few petals off.)* … while you said, 'He loves me, he loves me not, he loves me, he loves me not'? Human love can fail – we can let each other down or say unkind things. But today we remember that God will always love us. With God, it is always, 'He loves me. He loves me. He loves me.' *(Pull some more petals out as you say the words.)*

Second song

We're going to sing a song that you may have sung in Sunday school many years ago – 'Jesus loves me, this I know, for the Bible tells me so'. *(See appendix I, page 112. Sing the chorus several times if it's going well.)*

Prayers

Thank you, Lord God, that you are a compassionate and gracious God, slow to anger, abounding in love and faithfulness. Thank you that your love for each one of us will never fail. Amen

We'll say together the Lord's Prayer *(see appendix III, page 125–26)*.

Blessing

May God's blessing surround you each day,
as you trust him and walk in his way.
May his presence within guard and keep you from sin.
Go in peace, go in joy, go in love.

(Possible extra craft activity: the residents could be helped to write their names on individual card hearts, which could then be stuck on a poster or placed in a basket – a reminder that they are loved and precious to others and to God.)

Sample service 2 – God's wonderful world

For this service, you will need:

- *Some very beautiful fresh flowers*
- *YouTube clip of 'What a wonderful world'*
- *Song words (and music if possible) for 'All things bright and beautiful*

Setting the scene

If possible, set up a table and cloth with some flowers, a battery-powered candle, a Bible, and a cross, if you have one.

Opening words

We're going to have a short worship service now. I will switch on the candle to remind us that God is here with us. Jesus said, 'Where two or three are gathered together in my name, there am I in the midst of them' (Matthew 18:20, KJV).

In our service, we're going to think about the beauty of creation and give thanks to God, who made our beautiful world. Here's a song which talks about some of the things we might enjoy in our wonderful world.

Song

Play a YouTube clip of Louis Armstrong singing 'What a wonderful world'. Alternatively, you may like to find the lyrics online and read them out.

Bible reading

Today, we thank God who made this wonderful world. Here are some verses from Psalm 104 that help us to do that – perhaps you can picture the mountains and waterfalls, the birds and animals, the moon and the sun as I read the words.

Praise the Lord, my soul.

Lord my God, you are very great;
  you are clothed with splendour and majesty...

He makes springs pour water into the ravines;
  it flows between the mountains.
They give water to all the beasts of the field;
  the wild donkeys quench their thirst.
The birds of the sky nest by the waters;
  they sing among the branches.
He waters the mountains from his upper chambers;
  the land is satisfied by the fruit of his work.
He makes grass grow for the cattle,
  and plants for people to cultivate –
  bringing forth food from the earth...
He made the moon to mark the seasons,
  and the sun knows when to go down...

How many are your works, Lord!
  In wisdom you made them all...
I will sing to the Lord all my life;
  I will sing praise to my God as long as I live.

PSALM 104:1, 10–14, 19, 24, 33

Hymn

'All things bright and beautiful'. It would be good to print the words (see appendix I, page 109) out for the residents, although some who are unable to read or follow the words may well remember the chorus. If singing is difficult or you don't have music, try reading the words aloud.

Reflect

Take a few lovely flowers out of the vase on the table. Staff can show these around to individual residents, allowing time for them to touch, smell, and comment. Encourage a sense of appreciation of the beauty in the detail of the flowers.

Prayers

> We thank you, God, for the beauty of your creation. Thank you for the sun, moon, and stars; for the mountains and rivers and for the detail in tiny flowers and birds. Thank you for the joy these things bring us. We praise you, creator God. And we are sorry that we haven't always looked after your world. Help us to take care of it and to appreciate it. Amen.

Now we'll say together the Lord's Prayer *(see appendix III, page 125–26)*. Let us finish with a blessing, from Numbers:

> The Lord bless you
>   and keep you;
> the Lord make his face shine on you
>   and be gracious to you;
> the Lord turn his face towards you
>   and give you peace.
> NUMBERS 6:24–26

(Possible extra activity: if you are doing this service in the autumn, collect some conkers, attach each to a piece of string, then have a game of conkers with some of the residents. This is a good activity for encouraging reminiscences. Show the residents some conkers and acorns, then marvel at how these can become huge chestnut and oak trees. They speak of God's amazing creative powers, seen in nature. Possible extra hymn – 'Amazing grace', see page 111).

Sample service 3 – Peace in anxious times

For this service, you will need: song words and a YouTube clip of 'When peace like a river'.

Setting the scene

If possible, set up a table and cloth with some flowers, a battery-powered candle, a Bible, and a cross, if you have one.

Opening words and introduction

We have come together as the family of God in our Father's presence to offer him praise and thanksgiving, to hear and receive his holy word, to bring before him the needs of the world, to ask him to forgive our sins, and to seek his grace, that through his Son Jesus Christ, we may give ourselves to his service.

The theme of our service today is peace. But sometimes we don't feel at peace – we feel troubled in our minds or hearts.

I wonder what makes you feel anxious? *(Allow time for some to respond or give some suggestions.)* Do you worry about your health, or someone in your family? Maybe you worry about not being able to do something? Do you worry about the state of the world – perhaps the poor starving children or refugees? Sometimes it's at night-time that we find ourselves getting very anxious. We all know what it feels like to have very real worries and fears. Today, we think about God giving us his peace when we feel anxious.

Bible reading

I wonder if you've ever been seasick? Perhaps you were on a ferry crossing and the sea was really rough. Our Bible reading tells of the occasion when Jesus' disciples found themselves in a terrible storm on the Sea of Galilee. Perhaps you can imagine them in the boat.

That day when evening came, [Jesus] said to his disciples, 'Let us go over to the other side'... A furious squall came up, and the waves broke over the boat, so that it was nearly swamped. Jesus was in the stern, sleeping on a cushion. The disciples woke him and said to him, 'Teacher, don't you care if we drown?'

He got up, rebuked the wind and said to the waves, 'Quiet! Be still!' Then the wind died down and it was completely calm.

MARK 4:35, 37–39 (NIV)

Reflect

Imagine Jesus fast asleep while his friends were terrified and desperately trying to keep the boat from filling with water and overturning! It must have felt as if Jesus didn't care... but he was there all the time. When they cried out to him, they witnessed an amazing miracle as he rebuked the storm – 'Quiet! Be still!' – and it became completely calm.

The 'storms of life' that we experience can trouble us and upset us, making us feel anxious. And although we might not see immediate change in our circumstances, it helps to know that Jesus is with us *in* the storm, just as he was with the disciples. Giving our worries and fears to God makes a difference. The Bible says, 'Cast all your anxiety on [God] because he cares for you' (1 Peter 5:7). In our prayers now, we are going to ask for his peace.

Prayers

Teach the residents this prayer response. Every time you say, 'Dear Lord', they can join with you in saying, 'Give me your peace.' Practise a couple of times before starting the prayers.

Dear Lord,

All: Give me your peace.

When I am anxious about my health, dear Lord,

All: Give me your peace.

When I am worried about my loved ones, dear Lord,

All: Give me your peace.

When I fear the future, dear Lord,

All: Give me your peace.

When I feel troubled during the night, dear Lord,

All: Give me your peace.

In all the storms of life, help me to remember that you are with me, dear Lord,

All: Give me your peace.

Now we'll say together the Lord's Prayer *(see appendix III, page 125–26)*.

Hymn

We're going to sing an old hymn, 'When peace like a river', which includes the refrain, 'It is well with my soul'. This hymn was written in the 19th century by a man whose four young daughters had just died in a tragic drowning. Despite his terrible sadness and loss, he still was able to experience God's peace. *(Hand out the words if you have them and play the music from YouTube.)*

> When peace like a river, attendeth my way,
> when sorrows like sea billows roll;
> whatever my lot, thou hast taught me to say,
> 'It is well, it is well with my soul.'

It is well, with my soul,
It is well, with my soul,
It is well, it is well, with my soul.

Though Satan should buffet, though trials should come,
let this blest assurance control:
that Christ has regarded my helpless estate,
and hath shed his own blood for my soul.

Blessing

The peace of God, which passes all understanding, keep your hearts and minds in the knowledge and love of God and of his Son Jesus Christ our Lord; and the blessing of God Almighty, the Father, the Son, and the Holy Spirit, be among you and remain with you always. Amen.

Go round the group and bless each resident by name: 'Thelma, may you know God's peace… Freda, may you know God's peace… Abdul, may you know God's peace… Giselle, may you know God's peace…' and so on.

Appendix VI: Sample memorial services

The below services were put together by Anna Chaplain Margaret Hollands and are used with permission.

> Jesus said to her, 'I am the resurrection and the life. The one who believes in me will live, even though they die; and whoever lives by believing in me will never die.'
> JOHN 11:25–26

Sample service 1

Opening prayer

Dear God, thank you for *[insert name]* and for all they meant to me and to others. I have not been able to say goodbye to *[insert name]* with my family and friends as I would want to or be at the funeral. I ask you to be with *[insert name]*, and with those able to attend and those taking the service for us. Amen.

Bible reading

> The Lord is my shepherd, I lack nothing.
>   He makes me lie down in green pastures,
> he leads me beside quiet waters,
>   he refreshes my soul.
> He guides me along the right paths
>   for his name's sake.

Even though I walk
  through the darkest valley,
I will fear no evil,
  for you are with me;
your rod and your staff,
  they comfort me.

You prepare a table before me
  in the presence of my enemies.
You anoint my head with oil;
  my cup overflows.
Surely your goodness and love will follow me
  all the days of my life,
and I will dwell in the house of the Lord
  forever.
PSALM 23

You may like to reflect on your memories of *[insert name]*. Think about their life and all the things they enjoyed; remember all the times you spent together and the things you did together and with the wider family.

You may like to listen to some music that they liked or that was special to you or the family.

Prayers

Start with the Lord's Prayer *(see appendix III, page 125–26)*.

As *[insert name]* is committed into God's care, we pray: Heavenly Father, we thank you for all those whom we love but see no longer. As we remember *[insert name]* and all those who have gone before us, be with all those who mourn the death of a loved one. Amen.

Poems

Their light shines on

Our loved ones leave behind a light
That will never dim or fade
It's kept bright by the love we feel
And the memories we made.

It can warm us like a candle's glow
And help bring comfort too
And no matter where you go, you'll find
It's always close to you.

And in the darker time, remember –
In our hearts their light is strong
So every time we think of them
Their memory still shines on.

Life is but a stopping place

Life is but a stopping place, a pause in what's to be,
A resting place along the road, to sweet eternity.
We all have different journeys, different paths along the way.
We all are meant to learn some things, but never meant to stay…

Our destination is a place far greater than we know.
For some the journey's quicker; for some the journey's slow.
And when the journey finally ends, we'll claim a great reward,
And find an everlasting peace, together with the Lord.

Blessing

We ask for God's blessing on us all. May the Lord bring us his peace, may he comfort us by his Spirit, may he help us in every way through this time. May every tear that we shed bring us deeper healing, and may we know that *[insert name]* is safe in God's eternal care and reunited with those who have gone before. May the blessing of God, the Father, the Son, and the Holy Spirit be with us today and always. Amen.

Sample service 2

Before you find a place to sit quietly, you might like to find a photograph of *[insert name]*, write down some treasured memories, or play a special piece of music that connects you with them.

Think about those who are at the funeral and pray for them.

> Jesus said to her, 'I am the resurrection and the life. The one who believes in me will live, even though they die; and whoever lives by believing in me will never die.'
> JOHN 11:25–26

You might like to light a candle. Then pray:

> Be with us, loving God. Hear our prayers and comfort us in our loss, and help us to trust in your Son Jesus, whom you raised from the dead. Strengthen our faith and renew our hope that *[insert name]* and all those we love will share in his resurrection. Amen.

Remembering

Take some time now to reflect on ways that *[insert name]* was special to you. What things did you learn through their life and death, including about God?

Bible reading

The Lord is my shepherd, I lack nothing.
  He makes me lie down in green pastures,
he leads me beside quiet waters,
  he refreshes my soul.
He guides me along the right paths
  for his name's sake.
Even though I walk
  through the darkest valley,
I will fear no evil,
  for you are with me;
your rod and your staff,
  they comfort me.

You prepare a table before me
  in the presence of my enemies.
You anoint my head with oil;
  my cup overflows.
Surely your goodness and love will follow me
  all the days of my life,
and I will dwell in the house of the Lord
  forever.

PSALM 23

These words bring comfort that God, the good shepherd, is with us, even at the hardest of times, in the places of deepest darkness. When we feel anxious or troubled, God invites us to turn to him for help. This psalm also reminds us of the promise given that all who look to God in faith will dwell in his house forever.

Now give thanks to God for *[insert name]*'s life and ask for strength for yourself and those who grieve:

Loving God, thank you for *[insert name]* and for all that they meant to me and to others. *[Add your own thoughts here.]*

> I so wanted to say goodbye. Help me to know that you are there, holding all my hopes, holding all those I love, especially *[insert name]*, and holding me this day too. Be close to us all with your peace and hope. Amen.

> Heavenly Father, you have not made us for darkness and death, but for life with you forever. Without you, we have nothing to hope for; with you, we have nothing to fear. Speak to us now your words of eternal life. Lift us to the light and peace of your presence, and set the glory of your love before us today: through Jesus Christ our Lord. Amen.

Now pray this prayer, which is used at the end of an Anglican funeral service to say goodbye:

> God our creator and redeemer,
> by your power Christ conquered death
> and entered into glory.
> Confident of his victory
> and claiming his promises
> we entrust *[insert name]* to your mercy
> in the name of Jesus our Lord,
> who died and is alive
> and reigns with you,
> now and forever.
> Amen.

Appendix VII: Self-care exercises

Relaxation instructions

Lie down, make yourself comfortable, and relax as much as possible.

Arms

Now clench your right fist and build up the tension. Keep the rest of your body, apart from your fist and arm, as relaxed as possible. Then, stretch out your fingers, keep them stretched. Now relax your hand. Feel the tension going out of your hand as it relaxes. Now, while your right hand is relaxing, clench your left fist. Clench it tighter and tighter. Then, stretch the fingers of your left hand and hold the tension. Now relax your left hand. Feel the relaxation spreading through your hand.

Bend your right elbow and tense the upper part of your arm, feel the tension and hold it. Now let your arm relax and fall back into place. Focus on the relaxation in your arm. Now do that with your left arm. Bend your elbow and tense the upper part of your left arm, notice the tension and hold it. Now let the arm relax and fall back into place. Appreciate the relaxation in your arm.

This time push both arms straight out in front of you. Push them right out so that they're tense all the way along. Feel the tension, hold it. Relax your arms. Let your arms fall back comfortably and lie there. Feel how relaxed they've become and try to let them relax even further. Learn to recognise the difference between a tense and relaxed hand and arm. Let your arms just lie, relaxing.

Legs

Stay comfortable, with your arms relaxed. Lift your right leg up. The weight of gravity will cause the tension to build up. Hold your right leg in position and feel the tension building up. Now let it drop. Feel your leg and hips becoming relaxed as your foot rests on the ground. Notice the difference between your tense and relaxed leg. Now do the same with your left leg – lift it up. Hold it – let the tension build up. Now let it drop and feel both legs relaxing. Let your whole body relax. Let your legs, calves, and hips feel heavier and heavier as they relax.

Stomach and lower back

Pull your stomach in to contract your stomach muscles. You will find you cannot breathe easily. Hold it. You may find your chest and shoulders tightening as well. Now let go. Breathe normally again. Feel the relaxation spreading through your stomach, lower back, and chest.

Back and shoulders

Stay comfortable and relaxed. Now push your back up as though you are trying to raise your shoulders as high as possible. Let the tension build up. Feel and recognise the tension, hold it. Now let the tension go. Roll your shoulders. Feel the relaxation spreading through your shoulders and back. Just enjoy relaxing.

Neck

Stay comfortable and relaxed. Push your head back as far as you can. Feel the tension in your neck and keep it there. Keep pushing your head back. Notice the tension in your neck. Now let the tension in your neck go. Let it relax and fall back; appreciate the relaxation in it. This time, push your head forward so that your chin drops towards your chest. Press your chin towards your chest and feel the tension in the back of your neck. Hold that tension. Relax. Let your head fall back and rest comfortably and enjoy the relaxed feelings in your body.

Face

Stay comfortable and relaxed. Now press your tongue against the roof of your mouth. Hold the tension, then let it go. This time clench your teeth. Feel the tension in your jaw muscles. Hold the tension, and then let your jaw relax. Close your eyes tight shut; really press them shut. Hold the tension, and then stop screwing your eyes up and let them relax. Feel the relaxation spreading through your face.

Now concentrate on your forehead. Frown, making furrows in your brow. Hold that tension, and then let it go. This time, lift your eyebrows so high that your eyes open wide. Hold the tension. Let it go. Appreciate how relaxed your face is and try to let it relax even more. Feel the relaxation spread through your face. Notice the difference between your tense face and your relaxed face.

Whole-body

Now let your whole body feel more and more relaxed. You've relaxed each part of it. Now focus on each part of your body, making it more and more relaxed. Think about your hands. Feel them getting heavier and heavier. Let the heaviness spread up your arms and into your shoulders. Now the heaviness and relaxation is spreading down your back, into your hips and thighs, calves and legs, and feet. Now relax your face. Your whole body is feeling more and more relaxed.

Breathing

As you lie there, notice that your breathing has become slower. Take a deep breath. Hold the breath, then very slowly let it out. As you let it out, you will feel your body relax. Now do it again: take another deep breath, hold it, and then slowly let it out, relaxing as you do so. Lie there for a moment or two breathing in, and then relax as you slowly breathe out. You can always become more relaxed by taking a deep breath and slowly letting it out, and then by breathing slowly and deeply.

Realise that you can control the tension in your body, that you can relax it when you want to. Realise you can do this at any time you need to. If a part of your body feels tense, you can relax it when you want to. Stay in that position, relaxing. Just enjoy being totally relaxed.

Mindfulness exercise

1 Sit in a comfortable position and either close your eyes or rest them gently on a fixed spot in the room.
2 Visualise yourself sitting beside a gently flowing stream with leaves floating along the surface of the water. Pause for ten seconds.
3 For the next few minutes, take each thought that enters your mind and place it on a leaf… let it float by. Do this with each thought – pleasurable, painful, or neutral. Even if you have joyous or enthusiastic thoughts, place them on a leaf and let them float by.
4 If your thoughts momentarily stop, continue to watch the stream. Before long, your thoughts will start up again. Pause for 20 seconds.
5 Allow the stream to flow at its own pace. Don't try to speed it up and rush your thoughts along or 'get rid' of them. You are allowing them to come and go at their own pace.
6 If your mind says, 'This is pointless,' 'I'm bored,' or 'I'm not doing this right,' place those thoughts on leaves, too, and let them pass. Pause for 20 seconds.
7 If a leaf gets stuck, allow it to hang around until it's ready to float by. If the thought comes up again, watch it float by another time. Pause for 20 seconds.
8 If a difficult or painful feeling arises, simply acknowledge it. Say to yourself, 'I notice this feeling of boredom/impatience/frustration.' Place those thoughts on leaves and allow them to float along.
9 From time to time, your thoughts may hook you and distract you from being fully present in this exercise. This is normal. As soon as you realise that you have become sidetracked, gently bring your attention back to the visualisation exercise.

Summarised from 'Leaves on a stream' technique in Russ Harris, *ACT Made Simple: An easy-to-read primer on acceptance and commitment therapy* (New Harbinger, 2009), p. 113, used with kind permission (**newharbinger.com**).

Appendix VIII: Sample working agreement

Sample working agreement between a care home and the local church

Anna Chaplain: 'Jane Smith'

Care Home: 'Acacia Lodge'

Church: 'St Peter's Church'

Minister: 'The Revd Penny Thomas'

Spiritual Care

> Spiritual well-being enhances and integrates all other dimensions of health, including the physical, mental, emotional, and social... A person's spirituality is not separate from the body, the mind or material reality, for it is their inner life... It brings a sense of peace, harmony and conviviality with all.
>
> 'Spiritual Care Matters: An introductory resource for all NHS Scotland staff', NHS Scotland, 2009

Anna Chaplaincy

[St Peter's] Church appointed [Jane Smith] as Anna Chaplain to offer person-centred spiritual care on behalf of the church to older people in the local community. She has been trained for this work, and [St Peter's] has put in place DBS checks and safeguarding training.

Anna Chaplains offer support to older people living in their own homes and care homes, whatever their beliefs, by being a compassionate listening ear, supporting them with conversations around changing circumstances or end of life care. They can also support those who wish to continue to practise their personal Christian spirituality.

Visiting patterns

[Jane Smith] will visit [Acacia Lodge] as Anna Chaplain on [Thursday mornings], to offer:

General activities:

- Service in the lounge once a month for any resident, staff member, or visitor to attend if they would like to. *(May include Holy Communion.)*
- Seasonal services, including at Easter, Harvest, and Christmas.
- Group sessions in the lounge, including singing old songs and games.

Individual visits:

- Communion in residents' rooms where they cannot attend the communal service or for those who wish to receive it on their own.
- Availability to speak with and spend general time with anyone who is bedbound and would appreciate a visit.
- Praying and reading scriptures or daily reflections with those who would like Christian spiritual support.
- Attending those who are at the end of life and praying with them, as requested.
- Availability to talk with and support staff and family members when requested, especially around times of bereavement or supporting residents through end-of-life care.

Other notes

- An Anna Chaplain may at times need to speak with a resident in private so they feel comfortable enough to speak confidentially. Under safeguarding guidance, they would disclose anything relevant to either the care home manager or local minister as appropriate.

- The Anna Chaplain is able to visit anyone who requests a visit, anyone who already has a link with a local church, or whose family member requests a visit on their behalf.
- Being an Anna Chaplain is a voluntary role. [Jane] will try to keep to regular visiting times to give routine to residents but on occasion this may not be possible. She will inform the home as soon as possible if she is unable to attend.

The home will:

- Allocate members of staff to assist residents with mobility needs in getting to services and activities with the Anna Chaplain, reminding residents in the morning when a service is taking place, if appropriate.
- Make sure members of staff are in the room with the Anna Chaplain during services and activities to assist residents as needed.
- If possible, provide a room where interruptions can be kept to a minimum during services. Residents who do not want to attend are offered an alternative space in which to spend the duration of the service, so they are not forced to join in when this is against their beliefs and wishes.
- Allow the resident to spend time with the Anna Chaplain in private, if a confidential visit has been requested. Following safeguarding/lone-working guidelines, they will always leave the door to the resident's room open and make the Anna Chaplain aware of the nearest call bell, should assistance be required.
- Inform the Anna Chaplain if a resident they visit is unwell or dies, so they can offer any additional support needed to residents, staff, or family members.
- Contact the Anna Chaplain if the resident has requested a visit outside their normal visiting hours. If this is urgent, the Anna Chaplain will try to accommodate the request but may ask [The Revd Thomas] to attend on their behalf if unable to attend in person.
- Inform the Anna Chaplain if there is an infectious disease in the home, so they can take all necessary precautions or not attend, following the home's policies and guidance.

Signed: Date:
Anna Chaplain

Signed: Date:
Local minister

Signed: Date:
Care home manager:

To be reviewed annually.

Appendix IX: Regulatory requirements in meeting spiritual and religious needs

Each nation of the UK has its own regulatory framework for health and social care under which care homes are inspected. These are:

- Care Inspectorate Wales
- Care Inspectorate and Healthcare Improvement Scotland
- The Regulation and Quality Improvement Authority (Northern Ireland)
- Care Quality Commission (England)

In searching for standards that have a bearing on faith and spirituality, we might pick out references to 'things that matter to the person' or 'purposeful activities', and to faith, culture, and indeed human rights. Few explicit references can be found to 'spirituality' or 'spiritual needs' in the current requirements; however, both are implied where the wishes and voice of the service user are mentioned and where personalised care which respects the individual is expected.

Wales

Many of the regulations used by Care Inspectorate Wales have a bearing on spiritual and religious care. Regulations 14, 15, and 18 refer directly to religious and spiritual needs.

Regulation 14 concerns the 'suitability of the service'. In assessing whether the service is suitable for an individual, consideration must be given to whether or not religious and spiritual needs can be met, following which:

> 'In the case of adults, confirmation is provided in writing to the individual that the service can meet the individual's care and support needs including health, personal care, emotional, social, cultural, religious and spiritual needs. Confirmation in writing is provided where the service is unable to meet the individual's care and support needs.'

Regulation 15 covers the 'personal plan' created for new service users. The plan is to be co-produced with the person, and it sets out, among other things:

> 'How the individual will be supported to achieve their personal outcomes; How the individual's wishes, aspirations, and religious beliefs will be supported.'

Regulation 18 covers the 'provider assessment' which should be in place within seven days of the commencement of care. Needs it should identify include:

> 'Their personal preferences (taking into account any religious or philosophical beliefs or cultural background) and how these can be achieved.'

Northern Ireland

The minimum standards for care homes in Northern Ireland set out principles and expectations for good care.

Under Standard 2, 'Contact with family, friends and the local community is facilitated for residents.' Community includes church groups. Under this standard, we find the following guidance:

> '2:1 – Each resident is encouraged and facilitated to maintain, as far as possible, their existing links with family, friends and the local community.'

> '2:6 – Residents are consulted about visits by community groups and volunteers and the manager or senior member of staff on duty monitors these visits to ensure they benefit residents.'

Standard 5 says: 'Each resident has an up-to-date assessment of their needs.' Listed under the needs assessed are:

> 'The resident's physical, social, emotional, psychological and spiritual needs.'

> 'Specific needs and preferences if the resident is from a minority group.'

Standard 13 says: 'The home offers a structured programme of varied activities and events, related to the statement of purpose and identified needs of residents.' It specifies:

> '13:2 – The programme includes activities that are enjoyable, purposeful, age and culturally appropriate and takes into account the residents' spiritual needs.'

Standard 14 says: 'The death of a resident is respectfully handled as they would wish.' This includes:

> '14:4 – Arrangements are in place so that spiritual care can be made available for residents who are dying, if they so wish.'

> '14:6 – The body of a deceased resident is handled with care and respect and in accordance with his or her expressed social, cultural and religious preferences.'

Standard 26 says: 'Volunteers contribute to the home in the best interests of the residents.' This could include volunteers visiting from a local church. The standard specifies:

> '26.3 – Residents and staff are informed about individual volunteer's roles and responsibilities.'

> '26.4 – The scope of activity and responsibilities of each volunteer is specified in writing.'

Scotland

The Health and Social Care Standards for Scotland are underpinned by descriptive statements under five principles which are based on the outcomes service users should expect. These are the five principles:

1. Dignity and respect
2. Compassion
3. Be included
4. Responsive care and support
5. Well-being

Statement 1 says: 'I experience high quality care and support that is right for me.' Under the principle of dignity and respect in this statement, we read:

> '1.1 – I am accepted and valued whatever my needs, ability, gender, age, faith, mental health status, race, background or sexual orientation.'

Under compassion, the standards say:

> '1.7 – I am supported to discuss significant changes in my life, including death or dying, and this is handled sensitively.'

Where Statement 1 deals with eating and drinking under well-being, it states:

> '1.37 – My meals and snacks meet my cultural and dietary needs, beliefs and preferences.'

Statement 2 says: 'I am fully involved in all decisions about my care and support.'

Under well-being this statement says:

> '2.22 – I can maintain and develop my interests, activities and what matters to me in the way that I like.'

England

In 2024 the Care Quality Commission in England published new regulatory requirements and assessment guidelines. Under the new areas of questioning this new single assessment framework asks if services are:

1. Safe
2. Effective
3. Caring
4. Responsive to people's needs
5. Well-led

There are quality statements under each of these headings, and I-statements reflecting the outcomes service users wish to see. There are multiple references to protected equality characteristics, under the Equality Act 2010. For instance, the quality statement under 'Effective' says:

> 'People and communities have the best possible outcomes because their needs are assessed. Their care, support and treatment reflects these needs and any protected equality characteristics.'

Under 'Caring', a section on 'Treating people as individuals' has the following quality statement:

> 'We treat people as individuals and make sure their care, support and treatment meets their needs and preferences. We take account of their strengths, abilities, aspirations, culture and unique backgrounds and protected characteristics.'

This means:

> 'People's personal, cultural, social and religious needs are understood and met.'

The I-statement linked to this statement includes:

> 'I can keep in touch and meet up with people who are important to me, including family, friends and people who share my interests, identity and culture.'

Similarly, under 'Independence, choice and control', I-statements reflect spirituality, faith, and culture:

> 'I can keep in touch and meet up with people who are important to me, including family, friends and people who share my interests, identity and culture.'
>
> 'I am treated with respect and dignity.'
>
> 'I have care and support that enables me to live as I want to, seeing me as a unique person with skills, strengths and personal goals.'

Under 'Responsive to people's needs', there are statements about the importance of equity in allowing those who access care less easily due to protected characteristics to have equal access to provision of services, with barriers to their rights, and discrimination, being removed.

In considering 'Planning for the future', the quality statement says:

> 'We support people to plan for important life changes, so they can have enough time to make informed decisions about their future, including at the end of their life.'

This means:

> 'People who may be approaching the end of their life are identified (including those with protected characteristics under the Equality Act and people whose circumstances may make them vulnerable). This information is shared with other services and staff.'

Offering spiritual care in later life

About Anna Chaplaincy

Our network of Anna Chaplains offers spiritual care in later life, in a wide range of contexts. Named after the widow Anna in Luke's gospel, Anna Chaplains accompany older people in reflecting on their life and their relationship with God, breaking down generational barriers and offering prayerful presence and community.

Former broadcaster Debbie Thrower founded Anna Chaplaincy in Alton in 2010 and Anna Chaplaincy has been part of BRF Ministries since 2014. It is now led by Debbie Ducille. The network of Anna Chaplains is growing rapidly across the UK and the ministry is increasingly recognised as modelling compassionate, person-centred spiritual care for older people, as well as offering excellent training for aspiring Anna Chaplains, churches and communities.

BRF Ministries is the home of spiritual care in later life

For people of strong, little or no faith. Where everyone can find support and advocacy in later life and embrace their spirituality. A place to reflect on life lived and opportunities still to come. Where faith and fulfilment can thrive. And where it's never too late to find new meaning. We call it Anna Chaplaincy.

What Anna Chaplaincy offers

Network

The Anna Chaplaincy network numbers almost 500 Anna Chaplains across the UK, and it is growing rapidly as more and more churches discover all that the ministry has to offer. Anna Chaplains value belonging to the network and the opportunities it provides for support, sharing experience, learning and building community.

Training and events

Anna Chaplaincy offers a wide range of training events and day conferences, as well as an annual gathering for the network. The online, six-week Anna Chaplaincy training course is currently offered several times a year.

In addition, network get-togethers, regional gatherings and themed workshops are regularly held for Anna Chaplains and Friends, exploring pertinent topics such as end-of-life care, creating dementia-inclusive worship spaces and self-care. We also run regular introductory sessions to learn about becoming an Anna Chaplain.

Find out more at **annachaplaincy.org.uk/training-and-support**

Website

The Anna Chaplaincy website is a valuable resource in its own right, detailing all that the ministry has to offer, including resources, ideas for individuals and churches, and the vision that underpins it. A regular blog keeps readers abreast of current developments in spiritual care for older people and helps build a strong sense of community within the network.

Resources

Keen to establish and maintain good practice, Anna Chaplaincy has a strong training emphasis and offers a range of resources, including the acclaimed *Anna Chaplaincy Handbook* (see below), the Church Guides and Easy Guides series, and *Grief Conversations*. There is also a range of downloadable worship material online, including resources to support those involved with or living with dementia.

Anna Chaplaincy Handbook

This definitive guide to Anna Chaplaincy is for individuals sensing a calling to this ministry and for church leaders exploring Anna Chaplaincy as an effective response to the ageing demographic. Across 25 chapters, the handbook describes the Anna Chaplaincy approach to ministry among older people. Case studies offer fresh possibilities for fostering community cohesion and enabling people in their later years to deepen their spiritual life. If you are interested in buying a copy, please email **annachaplaincy@brf.org.uk**.

> Anna Chaplaincy is a sensitive pastoral ministry and the trademark name and logo can only be used with permission from BRF Ministries. If your church is interested in exploring Anna Chaplaincy and Anna Friends (who support the chaplains) please email **annachaplaincy@brf.org.uk** to arrange to talk to a member of the national team.

The Spiritual Care Series

The Spiritual Care Series is a highly regarded, tried-and-tested, award-winning training course to help churches and care providers resource their work offering spiritual care in later life. It gives those supporting older people in churches and care settings the confidence, understanding and skills to provide effective holistic spiritual care. Over 99% of participants who responded to a recent survey would recommend it to others, with 95% saying the content was excellent or very good.

Professor John Swinton of the University of Aberdeen, a leading practitioner in the field of spiritual care for older people in the UK and vice president of BRF Ministries, has been involved in the development of the course.

Consisting of eight two-and-a-half-hour sessions designed for group learning, including video material, the course covers a range of essential skills, including reflective listening, and uses a mixture of learning styles. The Spiritual Care Series is also available to individuals through online Zoom courses, which run throughout the year.

The sessions:

1. Understanding the ageing journey
2. Spirituality in ageing
3. Good communication
4. The power of storytelling
5. Dementia
6. A new home and a new way of life
7. Loss, grief, death and dying
8. Roles, boundaries, and self-care

We offer a minimum six-user licence. Cost is £300 per initial course pack (six users) and includes two facilitator guides and six licences to access the Bridge online learning environment, where material is accesible and downloadable. Participants can order hard copies if desired, for an extra £19.99 each. We also offer it as a self-directed course for £80.

More information can be found at **annachaplaincy.org.uk/spiritual-care-series.**

About the authors

Julia Burton-Jones is training and development lead for Anna Chaplaincy at BRF Ministries, having developed Anna Chaplaincy in Kent for eleven years and worked previously as a dementia trainer in older people's care settings.

Catriona Foster was pastor for older people for 18 years at St John's Church in Harborne, Birmingham, before retiring in 2025, and was a founding member of the Anna Chaplaincy national network.

Following a career in journalism and broadcasting, **Debbie Thrower** pioneered Anna Chaplaincy in Alton in Hampshire from 2010 before joining the staff team at BRF Ministries in 2014 to develop Anna Chaplaincy as a national movement. She retired in 2024 as ministry lead but continues working for Anna Chaplaincy on a voluntary basis as a vice president for BRF Ministries.

After a career in nursing and nurse education, **the Revd Sally Rees** was ordained in the Church in Wales with a remit to develop older people's ministry in her ministry area and also given a diocesan role as bishop's officer for older people. She pioneered Anna Chaplaincy in Wales across several denominations, and on stepping down from this national role became a freelance trainer for Anna Chaplaincy at BRF Ministries and coordinator for Swansea and Brecon Diocese.

Six-session course handbook
Creative arts workshop
Sermon starters
Bible studies
Meditations
Prayer walk
A church's guide
to exploring mortality
Death
& Life
Joanna Collicutt
Jo Ind
Victoria Slater
Alison Webster

Inspiring people of all ages to grow in Christian faith

BRF Ministries is the home of Anna Chaplaincy, BRF Resources, Messy Church and Parenting for Faith

As a charity, our work would not be possible without fundraising and gifts in wills.
To find out more and to donate,
visit brf.org.uk/give or call +44 (0)1865 319700